D0777985

how to repair
SMALL APPLIANCES

by

JACK DARR

HOWARD W. SAMS & CO., INC.
THE BOBBS-MERRILL CO., INC.
INDIANAPOLIS · KANSAS CITY · NEW YORK

FIRST EDITION

TWELFTH PRINTING—1971

Copyright © 1961 and 1966 by Howard W. Sams & Co., Inc.,
Indianapolis, Indiana 46206. Printed in the United States of
America.

All rights reserved. Reproduction or use, without express per-
mission, of editorial or pictorial content, in any manner, is
prohibited. No patent liability is assumed with respect to the
use of the information contained herein. While every precaution
has been taken in the preparation of this book, the publisher
assumes no responsibility for errors or omissions. Neither is any
liability assumed for damages resulting from the use of the
information contained herein.

International Standard Book Number: 0-672-20041-4
Library of Congress Catalog Card Number: 61-10963

TABLE OF CONTENTS

CHAPTER 1

CHAPTER 2

CHAPTER 3

CHAPTER 4

CHAPTER 5

PREFACE

You can learn to repair small electrical appliances—either for your own benefit, or as a profitable sideline or full-time occupation. (I personally have found appliance servicing a profitable adjunct to my radio-TV servicing business.) At first glance, some appliances may seem complicated. Actually, they aren't. Take an electric iron, for example; it consists of a cord, heating element, thermostat, and chassis. Taking one apart is often tricky, but it can be done with a little know-how and patience.

Nor do you need expensive tools. Most readers will already have the necessary assortment of screwdrivers, wrenches, etc. Where to buy parts—always a stumbling block in appliance servicing—is also fully explained in this book.

As you'll learn, broken or worn line cords and plugs, and defective heating elements and thermostats, are the most common appliance troubles. Individual chapters have therefore been devoted to these subjects, as well as to electric motors. Once you learn how to replace a worn line cord or plug in a toaster, you should have no trouble replacing one in, say, an iron or a popcorn popper.

Information on handy tools, service techniques, and practical tips—gleaned from my experiences as owner of an electrical-electronic fix-it shop—will save you time and trouble in repairing any of the 15 appliances discussed in this book.

JACK DARR

CHAPTER 1

APPLIANCE CONSTRUCTION and OPERATION

The majority of household appliances are relatively simple, consisting of nothing more than a heating element, thermostat (a device to control heat), and perhaps a small electric motor. Appliances, like any other man-made equipment of this type, become defective from time to time. Such defects can cause them to operate improperly, or not at all. The trouble may be either mechanical or electrical, or both. Usually a repair job will consist of nothing more than replacing a line cord or plug, or maybe simply cleaning and lubricating a unit. Furthermore, disassembling some appliances—an electric iron, for example—is often more tricky than the actual repair.

Let's take a look at some of these devices, and see what makes them "tick."

TOASTERS

The first, and by all means one of the most popular household appliances, is the toaster. The simplest type is the old-fashioned toaster shown in Fig. 1-1. It consists of a heating element positioned in the center of a metal frame, three rods on each side to hold the bread away from the element, and two hinged doors which, when closed, place the bread in position

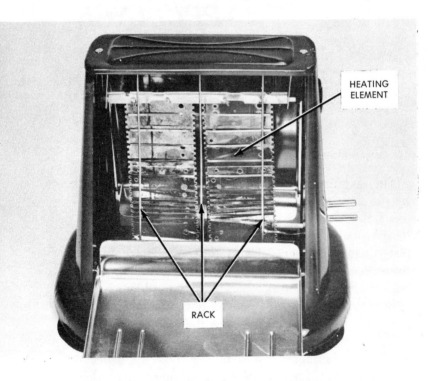

Fig. 1-1. Here is the simplest form of electric toaster—the manual type. The lids in each side lower as shown; the bread is placed against the rack, and the lids then released. Actually this unit consists of nothing but a heating element and a line cord.

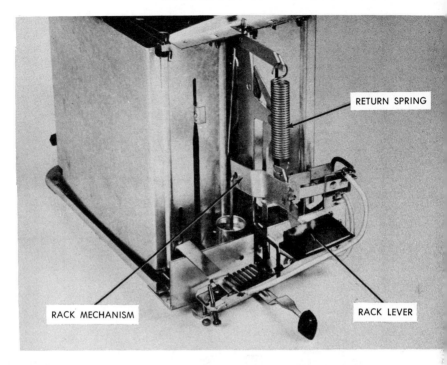

Fig. 1-2. The mechanism of an automatic toaster. Bread is placed on two racks inside, and the racks pushed down by the lever at the lower right. This not only latches the rack down, but also closes the switch that energizes the heating element and starts the timer.

for toasting. No thermostatic control is used; the bread is simply removed when the desired charring has taken place! Early toasters were relatively inexpensive and rarely caused trouble. When they did, it was due to a defective line cord or plug, or a burned-out heating element. Cords and plugs could be easily replaced, and so could heating elements, but a new toaster could be purchased for just a few dollars more. Anyway, it wasn't long before the automatic toaster was developed, eliminating the need for constant watching and the scraping of burnt toast to make it palatable.

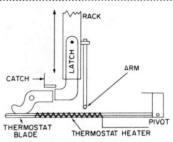

(A) Rack down; thermostat heater on.

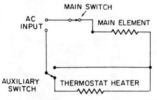

(B) Switch positions for the condition at A.

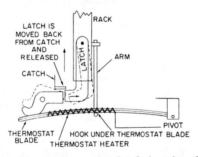

(C) Thermostat cools; latch is tripped.

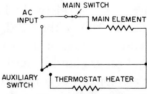

(D) Switch positions prior to tripping action.

Fig. 1-3. An electromechanical timing control.

In the automatic toaster, the bread is placed in a rack which slides down between separate heating elements. When the operating lever is depressed, a timing mechanism is started and the heating elements turned on for a predetermined length of time. A latch then releases the rack and it pops up, lifting the toast and opening the circuit to the heating element simultaneously. The mechanism is exposed in Fig. 1-2.

There are several versions of the timing mechanism, some quite complicated mechanically. One popular type uses a sort of "electromechanical" timing control. Refer to the drawings in Fig. 1-3; this is how it works:

1. The rack is pushed down by hand, causing the latch to engage the catch on the frame and hold the rack down (Fig. 1-3A). This action closes the main and auxiliary switches (Fig. 1-3B), allowing current to flow through the heating element wrapped around the bimetal blade of the thermostat. (When cold, this blade is straight.) Current now flows through both the thermostat heater and the main heating element.

2. The thermostat heater causes the bimetal blade to warp (Fig. 1-3C) and "bow up" in the center. When the blade reaches its maximum warp, the hook arm on the right side of the rack catches under the thermostat blade and holds it up. An extension on the hook arm (not shown) closes an auxiliary switch which bypasses the thermostat heater (Fig. 1-3D), leaving only the main element in the circuit.

3. Since current no longer flows through it, the thermostat heater cools off. The bimetal blade attempts to resume its normal straight form; however, since its center is held up by the hook arm, the left end rises, causing the trigger arm to push the latch away from the catch; and the rack pops

11

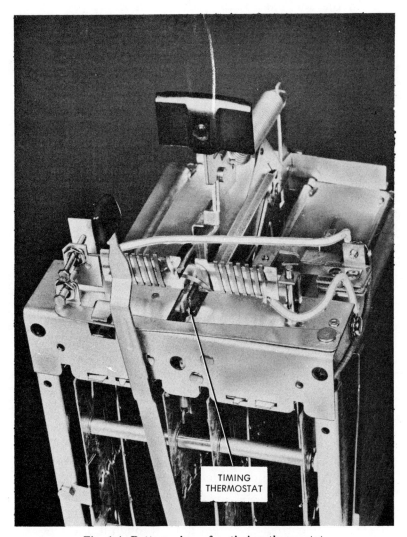

Fig. 1-4. Bottom view of a timing thermostat.

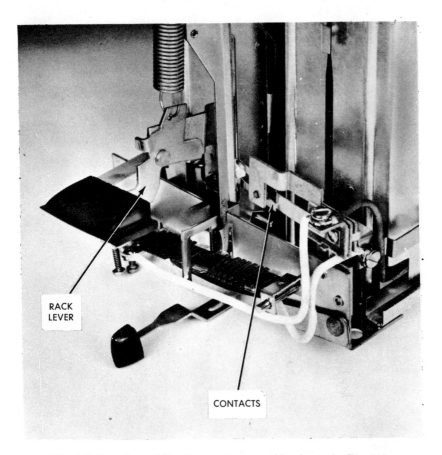

Fig. 1-5. Top view of the thermostat assembly shown in Fig. 1-4.

CLOCKWORK
TIMER

Fig. 1-6. An automatic toaster with a clockwork timer.

Fig. 1-7. Testing the toaster elements with an appliance tester. Meter readings can be used to check the continuity of elements, the condition of switch contacts, etc.

up. When this happens, the main switch is also opened. Fig. 1-4 shows the bottom view of the timing thermostat; the top view appears in Fig. 1-5.

Being an electromechanical device, the automatic toaster can be difficult to service. The first step toward correcting troubles is to see that all latch bars, triggers, and other arms and levers are perfectly free. If the toaster has been used for some time without being properly cleaned, it is highly possible that an accumulation of crumbs, butter, etc., may have fouled the mechanism. Much of the mechanical action depends on gravity; in other words, some of the arms and levers fall into place rather than being pulled by a spring. Thus, everything must move freely for proper action.

If their edges are worn, rounded, or bent, the trigger and latch bars will not work properly. All triggers should therefore be sharp-edged. If necessary, remove the offending piece and square up the engaging surfaces with a very small pattern file. Bent arms will often cause binding.

A second type of automatic toaster is shown in Fig. 1-6. It operates in much the same way as the first type, except its timing action is controlled by the small windup clockwork mechanism pointed out in the illustration. Pushing the operating lever down winds a small spring, latches the rack in position, and turns on the heating elements, all at the same time. When the clockwork has run down, the trigger is released, the rack pops up, and the heating elements are shut off. Operating time can be varied by setting an adjustment on the timer to provide the desired shade of toast. The black substance at the upper right of Fig. 1-6 is a special heat-resistance grease which provides the necessary lubrication. Occasional relubrication is called for. If heat-resistant grease is not available, use a silicone compound such as DC-4, which is not likely to melt and run because of heat.

The heating elements of any toaster can be quickly checked for continuity (a continuous electrical DC path) by using the appliance tester shown in Fig. 1-7. By plugging the toaster into the receptacle on the side and switching the instrument on, you can tell from the wattage reading if all elements are working. For instance, suppose the wattage rating shown on the toaster is 300 watts, and four individual elements are used (one on each side of the two racks). If the meter indicates a drain of only 225 watts, you can immediately diagnose the trouble as one open element. Another time-saving feature of such an appliance tester is that you can check the main-switch contacts without waiting for the elements to become red-hot. (A toaster is difficult to work on when its elements are hot!) Leave the toaster plugged into the wattmeter; an immediate reading indicates good contact, and no reading indicates switch trouble.

Automatic-toaster troubles can be classified into two distinct groups—doesn't work at all, or doesn't work right. The first is by far the easier to trace and repair; since none of the heating elements glow, it's obvious no current is reaching them. This is most often due to a defective line cord or plug (covered in Chapter 2), although one of the element switches may not be making proper contact, or in certain rare cases an open element may be the cause. Improper operation and the various causes can be further classified as follows:

1. Rack won't pop up, or won't stay down. Check mechanical action of all catches, levers, and latches. Clean and lubricate as necessary. Check thermostat or timer operation.

2. Timing adjustment doesn't work right. Check mechanical action; usually a good cleaning will restore normal operation.

3. One side doesn't toast properly. Inspect heating elements on both sides of rack; you'll probably find one that doesn't glow, indicating an open element (see Chapter 3).

SHAVERS

Electric shavers are quite common today, and although they vary in size, shape, and color, their principle of operation is basically the same. Most of the early models were of the vibrator type shown in Fig. 1-8, which operated from the 60-cycle electromagnetic field of a coil. Later models use a small synchronous or brush-commutator motor. The action is readily apparent as soon as the shaver is partially disassembled; and since motor operation and troubles are discussed in detail in a later chapter, we'll concern ourselves here with only the mechanical operation of typical shavers.

Fig. 1-9 shows a popular American shaver which has a three-speed motor. The speed-selector switch on the bottom of the case changes connections on the field coils to alter the motor speed. The motor itself is a variation of the synchronous type, with a dumbbell-shaped metal armature. Fig. 1-10 shows the shaver partially disassembled. The armature can be seen in the center of the housing, between the two field coils. The plastic blade-actuating lugs are at the bottom protruding through a foam pad used to deaden some of the motor noise. The motor drives an eccentric cam which is coupled to the blade-holding bracket. As the cam revolves, it moves the cutting heads back and forth under the combs. With the contacts closed, the electromagnetic field of the coil causes the armature to rotate. As the heavy portion reaches the field, the contacts open momentarily. Flywheel action keeps the armature going until the contacts close again. If the contacts should be open when the shaver is plugged in, a thumbwheel is used to spin the armature and start the motor.

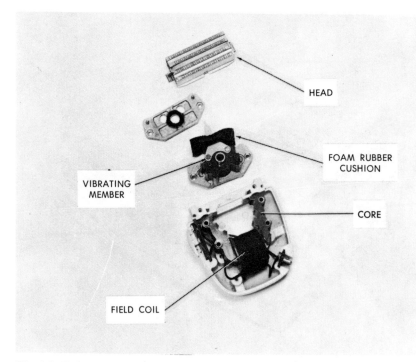

Fig. 1-8. Construction of an early electric shaver using a vibrator-type driving mechanism.

Disassembly of this shaver is simple: Loosen, *but do not remove*, the two screws at each end. The two on the bottom are visible, and the two at the top are under the shaving heads at the left. To reach the latter, open the two end caps and lift the shaving heads out of their clips; the screws can be seen on a flat metal plate under the foam pad. Each screw has a special fastener which hooks into recesses in the plastic case; one of these can be seen between the motor and lid, at the bottom of the picture.

When reassembling, be sure all four screws and fasteners are seated properly in their recesses before tightening them down. Two flat springs, under the metal

19

Fig. 1-9. A three-speed shaver. The arrow-shaped switch (at the bottom of the case) is the speed selector; the other one is the on-off switch.

plate at the top, hold the end caps; they must be in place and the end caps hooked under them before the final tightening adjustment is made. Be sure the case is fitted together properly before tightening the screws. The two halves must fit snugly; otherwise the plastic case will be strained and perhaps broken when the screws are tightened. Holding the end-cap springs may be a little tricky; to do so, grasp the shaver so the bottom rests in the heel of your hand, and place your fingers over the metal plate. Set the screws very loosely, making sure the case is put together properly. Snapping a heavy rubber band crosswise around the case will

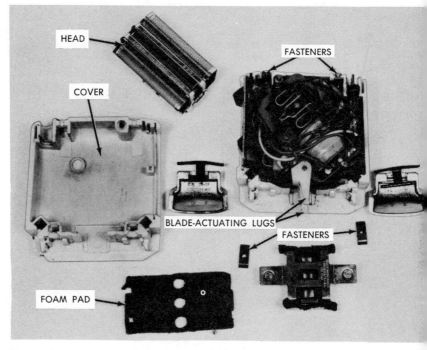

Fig. 1-10. The shaver in Fig. 1-9 disassembled. Notice the special fasteners which hold the case together.

help hold the case together until the tiny pieces are all in place.

A different type of shaver, using two rotary cutting heads driven by tiny gears, is shown partially disassembled in Fig. 1-11. This view shows the back of the motor, a brush-commutator type. The small ceramic capacitors at each end minimize radio and TV interference. The brushes can be seen at each side of the motor, in the small rectangular openings. Each brush slips down the guide and is held against the commutator by a straight wire spring in the brush holder.

Motor lubrication is essential for proper operation, but excess oil will tend to "gum up the works" by pick-

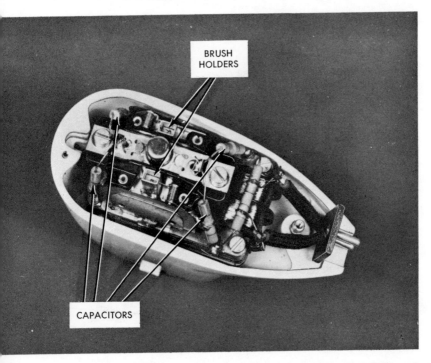

BRUSH
HOLDERS

CAPACITORS

Fig. 1-11. An imported electric shaver. Note the construction of
the motor. The small rectangular brush holders are visible on
each side of the motor, and four capacitors are employed to
minimize radio and television interference.

ing up tiny bits of hair, dust, etc. Use a very thin oil,
and put only one drop on each end of the shaft. To lubricate the cutting heads, rub one drop of oil between
your thumb and forefinger; then rub the parts to be
lubricated with your fingertip.

Most shaver troubles stem from worn or dirty shaving heads and blades, the usual complaint being that
the unit doesn't shave as smoothly or closely as it once
did. A good cleaning, and replacement of the shaving
heads, are usually all that are necessary. (The cutting
heads of many shavers can be sharpened with an abra-

sive compound. Instructions for this operation usually accompany the shaver.)

If the motor fails to operate at all, the connecting cord or plug is likely to be defective. Of course, there is always the possibility that something has gone wrong with the motor. Some motor defects can be repaired; if not, the motor will have to be replaced. (See Chapter 4 on motors.)

Sometimes the motor will run, but there will be no cutting action. Check the mechanical coupling between the motor armature and the blades or cutting heads. Invariably, you'll find some link disconnected and out of place.

IRONS

Actually, the electrical part of an iron is very simple—it consists of just a heating element and a thermostat. As with most small appliances, the complications arise in trying to take them apart. Each manufacturer resorts to a different method of assembling the pieces, and finding the key to the puzzle is often very time consuming.

Fig. 1-12 shows an older-type standard iron partly disassembled. A pair of slots at each end of the cover

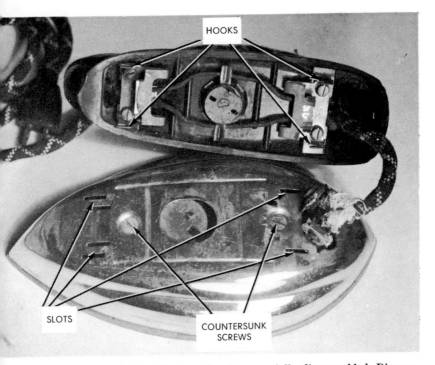

Fig. 1-12. An older-type dry iron partially disassembled. Dismantling an electric iron can be quite tricky unless you know the right "combination," as explained in the text.

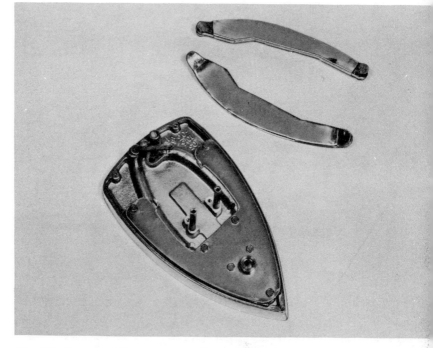

Fig. 1-13. Some typical replacement heating elements for electric irons.

(the chromium-plated shell which covers the element and bottom of the iron) engage the hooks pointed out on the bottom of the handle section. To disassemble this type of iron, lift the rear hooks by inserting a long screwdriver into the hole in the back of the handle, under the cord, and prying up the hook spring. When slid back and up, the handle then comes off. The cover can be removed, to reach the heating element and the thermostat, by unscrewing the two large countersunk screws on top.

Fig. 1-13 shows a selection of typical replacement elements for this iron. These elements are made of flat mica plates with flat resistance wire wound around

Fig. 1-14. A special iron tester is used. The iron is placed on the stand, and plugged into the AC outlet on the side. The thermometer reads the sole-plate temperature, and the pilot light glows when the iron is drawing current. The appliance tester at the right can be used to check current consumption.

them. The heating element at the bottom of the picture is a sealed-unit type in which connections are made by means of the terminal screws. The two-piece element at the upper right requires a jumper connection across the front of the iron; the thermostat and cord connect to the remaining terminals at the back.

For checking these and any other irons, the tester shown in Fig. 1-14 is very handy. It consists of a high-temperature thermometer which is read from the indicating scale on the front panel. The iron is plugged into a receptacle on the side of the instrument, and a pilot light indicates when it is drawing current.

The appliance tester at the right (shown previously) is handy for finding out how much current the element is drawing. This is done by checking the reading against the rating plate on the iron. For example, if the iron is rated at 1 kilowatt and the tester shows it is only drawing 700 watts, either the element is defective or the thermostat is not operating properly.

Steam Irons

Electrically there is no difference between a steam iron and a dry iron. The steam iron has a small reservoir

Fig. 1-15. A typical steam and dry iron. Water is poured into the reservoir through the hole in the handle, just below the variable-heat control.

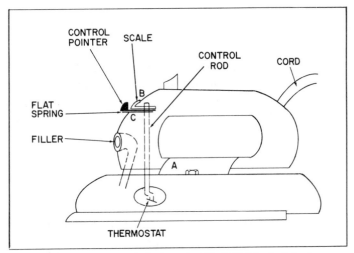

Fig. 1-16. Construction of the iron in Fig. 1-15. Study this diagram well; because of constant use and abuse, irons always seem to need fixing.

that can be filled with water. A control valve in the handle allows the water to drip slowly into recesses inside the soleplate. Here it is converted into steam which escapes through holes in the bottom of the soleplate, dampening the clothes as they are ironed. The iron may be used dry by simply closing the valve or pouring out the water.

A typical steam iron is pictured in Fig. 1-15, and Fig. 1-16 shows its construction. To disassemble:

1. Pry up curved aluminum cover A, exposing the large nut in the center of the cover. Remove the nut.

2. With your fingernail, pull temperature scale B and spring C straight forward and out. (In some models, the spring does not come all the way out.)

3. Pull the small aluminum collar (the funnel-like device marked "Fill Here" on the front of the

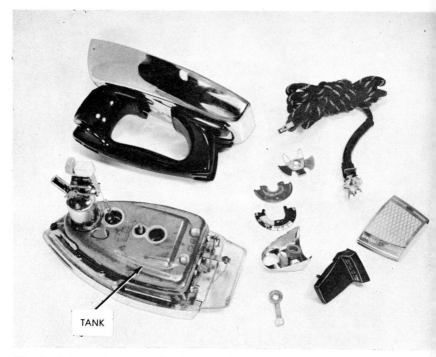

TANK

Fig. 1-17. The steam and dry iron in Fig. 1-15 disassembled. Notice the water tank, located beneath the cover.

handle) straight out. Be careful because the collar is easily bent.

4. Lift the handle straight up and off. Note very carefully the position of the control rod (the long, flat metal rod going from the control knob down to the thermostat).

5. Loosen, but do not remove, the two screws holding the spade lugs attached to the line cord.

To reassemble, reverse Steps 1 through 5. Be very careful not to use force because this assembly is delicate. If properly assembled, it will go back together with a minimum of forcing. (Note: When inserting the flat spring under the temperature scale, be sure the

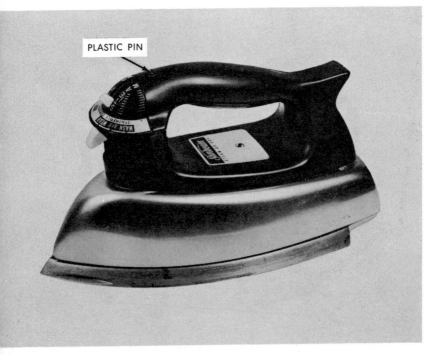

PLASTIC PIN

Fig. 1-18. Another popular steam and dry iron. The plastic pin
on top is your "key" to the insides of the iron.

prongs are turned *up* so they apply proper tension on
the scale.) Fig. 1-17 shows the iron disassembled.

Another type of steam iron is shown in Fig. 1-18.
Note carefully the small, round plastic pin on the front
of the handle, just behind the steam control. To disassemble this iron, drive the pin straight down inside the
handle. The scale, steam control, and other parts can
then be removed, and the pin recovered after the iron
has been taken apart. (If the top of the pin happens to
be sufficiently exposed, it can be pulled out.)

There are so many variations of fastenings that it is
impossible to provide specific rules for taking an iron
apart. The units shown are the most popular makes

and are representative of most irons. Two general rules, however, should always be followed: There will *always* be an easy way of taking the iron apart—the trick is to find it. First take out all visible fastenings; if the iron still doesn't come apart, start looking for some hidden key or trigger which will release the rest of the parts. (It's like the puzzles you used to work when you were a child, where pulling out the key piece let the rest of the pieces fall apart.)

The other, and perhaps more important, rule is *never* use force. Although the temptation may be great, resist it. The use of force will only damage some part which may take you two or three weeks to replace.

As a rule, the actual repair is almost absurdly simple—replacement of an element, bad thermostat, cord, plug, etc. Be sure the connections to the element are tight when replacing it. Because it carries a heavy current, a loose or dirty connection can become overheated and cause damage. Also burnish the contact points on the thermostats until they shine, in order to lessen arcing and extend contact life.

KNIFE SHARPENERS

Electric knife sharpeners like the one in Fig. 1-19 are extremely easy to service. With the cover removed as shown in Fig. 1-20, this model consists merely of a small motor, a switch, a fan, and two small grinding wheels. The brushes and commutator are located on the other side of the motor. The switch is a simple slide-type which is actuated by pushing down the plastic plate on top of the unit. A spring returns the switch to its off position so the motor cannot be left running accidentally.

Troubles in units like this stem from worn brushes, lack of lubrication, or faulty switch action. If the motor fails to run, check the switch, cord, plug, and all wiring connections to make sure power is reaching the motor. If you suspect motor trouble, refer to Chapter 4.

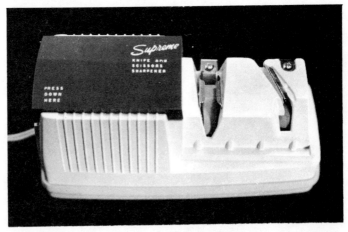

Fig. 1-19. Top view of a knife and scissors sharpener. The switch is activated by merely pressing down on the top plate, where marked.

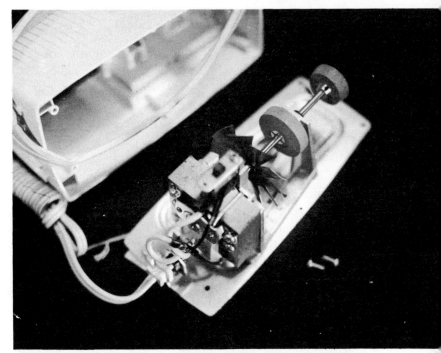

Fig. 1-20. Internal construction of the knife sharpener in Fig. 1-19. Not much can go wrong here, and the mechanism is easily accessible by removing six screws holding the cover.

MIXERS

Basically, there are two types of electric kitchen mixers, although they operate on exactly the same principle. The model in Fig. 1-21 is an example of a portable mixer. Its variable-speed motor drives a set of gears which turn the beaters.

Fig. 1-22 shows a disassembled view. The motor brushes are visible between the motor frame and gear box at the left. The gearing is simple, usually a worm gear mounted in the center of the box and driving two counterrotating pinions, one on each side.

Most mixer troubles are confined to bad line cords, plugs, and speed-control devices like the centrifugal governor discussed in the chapter on motors. Clean the machine, removing as much assorted flour, lint, dust, and the like as possible. Also clean the contacts of the speed control. Then relubricate the machine very sparingly (you don't want oil to dribble into the cake batter).

Bent or damaged beaters can sometimes be straightened, but they usually will have to be replaced . . . especially if—as one housewife told the author—she "stirred a spoon in with the mashed potatoes!"

For some reason, gear trouble is not as common as you might expect. The gear box is easily accessible on almost all machines; on the example shown, only four screws need be removed. Excessive grease leakage at the beater sockets may be a sign of worn bearings in the gear box. Broken gear teeth and similar troubles will be immediately obvious.

Speed-control switches, if of the tap-switch type, can be cleaned with a chemical contact cleaner. Brushes must be long enough and have ample spring tension to

Fig. 1-21. A small hand kitchen mixer. No stand is necessary. The beaters are removed by pressing in on the top front of the case, and the unit can be hung on a bracket (or nail) on the wall.

maintain good contact at all times. On the smaller mixers, the commutator and brushes are easily accessible. On the larger units, the insulated caps over the ends must be taken off before the brushes can be removed.

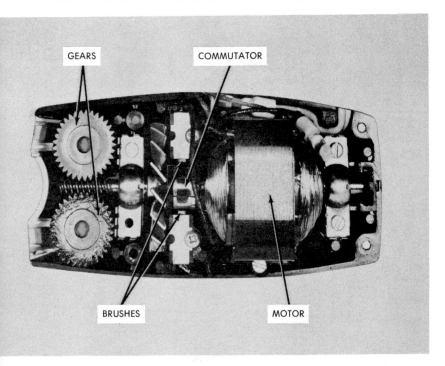

Fig. 1-22. A bottom view of the mixer in Fig. 1-21, with outer housing removed. Incidentally, only four screws need be removed to gain access to the underside of this model. The motor frame can be seen in the center, and the commutator and brushes are between the motor and gear box, at the left.

BLENDERS

The electric blender (Fig. 1-23) does the same job as the mixer, only in a different way. Food is placed in a glass or plastic container; and knives or blades mounted in the bottom, revolving at a high speed, chop it into a fine pulp.

Fig. 1-23. The electric blender does most of the things a mixer does, only faster.

37

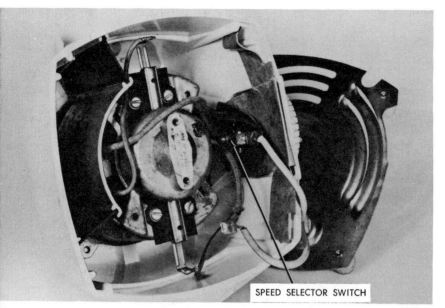

SPEED SELECTOR SWITCH

Fig. 1-24. Bottom view of the blender with the cover plate removed. This device is comprised mainly of a simple variable-speed motor, along with a splined socket to receive the drive spline of the knives in the bowl. The speed control can be seen at the side of the frame.

The knives are an integral part of the container and are mounted on a bearing at the bottom. When the container is placed on top of the motor, a spline engages an 8-point socket on top of the motor shaft. The blender is comparatively simple, as seen from the underside view in Fig. 1-24. This model has three speeds, selected by the switch on the side. The motor is larger than those in most other appliances, in order to force the knives through such heavy materials as raw meat.

Damaged knife blades are common, but they are easily replaced. Other typical troubles generally involve defective cords and switches. Motors are sometimes at fault, particularly when they have seen more than their share of "heavy" duty. (See Chapter 4 on motors.)

COFFEE MAKERS

Coffee makers, though varying in size, shape, and type, have essentially the same electrical system. Fig. 1-25 shows a typical wiring arrangement used in many of the automatic types. Practically all are thermostatically controlled, and are timed so that heat is applied for just the right amount of time to brew perfect coffee, as well as keep it warm afterward. Some have adjustable thermostats so that the coffee can be varied in strength by allowing it to boil or percolate for different lengths of time.

Fig. 1-26 shows some typical replacement heating elements. Those at the top of the photo are flat, or plate, types; those at the bottom are cylindrical. The plate type on the left is a sealed unit, whereas the one on the right is an older, wirewound resistance type on a mica form. The encased cylindrical types use the same type of resistance-wire heating element, but it is wound on a cylindrical mica or ceramic form mounted in the aluminum cylinders. The long bolt fastened to the cylinder case holds the element in place, as seen

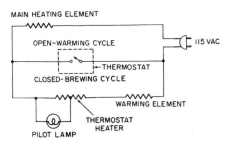

Fig. 1-25. The wiring arrangement used on many automatic coffee makers. The brewing cycle occurs when the thermostat is closed; the warming cycle, when it's open.

39

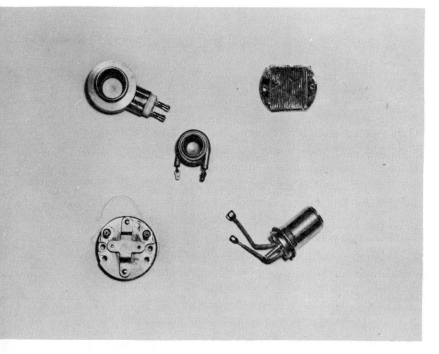

Fig. 1-26. Typical replacement heating elements for coffee makers. Notice the two types, cylindrical and flat. Some of these will fit quite a few different units; others are "special" and fit only those models for which they are designed.

in the bottom view of Fig. 1-27. The bolt and element are inserted from the top, and the bolt pulls the cylindrical case down tightly into the bottom of the pot. Be very careful, when handling these elements, not to dent or mar the rim—this can cause leaks when the element is installed.

Note the ceramic feedthrough insulators for the leads in Fig. 1-27. Be sure to replace them when reassembling the unit to prevent short circuits or accidental grounding.

Fig. 1-28 shows two thermostats used in the more elaborate automatic coffee makers. The unit on the right

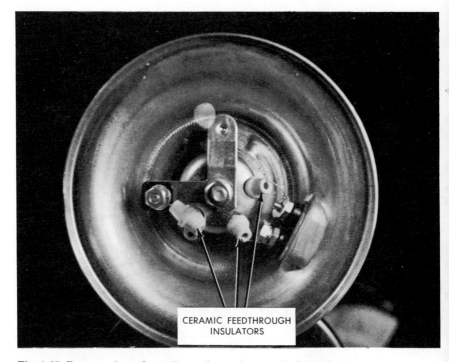

CERAMIC FEEDTHROUGH
INSULATORS

Fig. 1-27. Bottom view of a coffee maker using a cylindrical heat-ing element. The end of the long mounting bolt can be seen at the center. This bolt allows the element to be drawn down tightly against the bottom of the pot. The leads of the heating element are passed through holes which are insulated by ceramic beads.

is not adjustable, and it mounts in the base of the pot. The unit at the left can be adjusted by setting the lever extending at the lower right. This adjustment regulates the boiling time, and hence the strength of the coffee.

Now and then you may have to repair a leaky alu-minum pot or urn. Aluminum is always difficult to sol-der, but if you use a clean iron (do not use a gun) and a special flux sold under the trade name of *Sal-Met*, you'll be able to solder aluminum with comparative ease. The aluminum solder can then be filed smooth

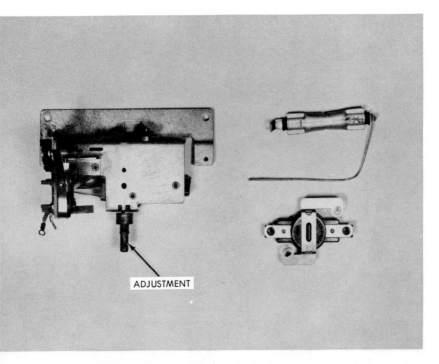

Fig. 1-28. Typical replacement thermostats for automatic coffee makers. The unit at the right is not adjustable. The one at left can be adjusted by moving the lever shown; this regulates the boiling time and hence the strength of the coffee.

and polished until it is indistinguishable from the rest of the pot.

POPCORN
POPPERS

The appliance shown in Fig. 1-29 is POPular, especially in the winter! This one is a simple version of an electric popcorn popper with an open-wire heating element (Fig. 1-30). Its heat is regulated so that just the proper amount is received for popping the corn without having to stir or shake it. Some of the more elaborate versions use thermostatic controls and sealed elements.

Fig. 1-29. An electric popcorn popper is actually a very simple device comprised of nothing more than a heating element and a container.

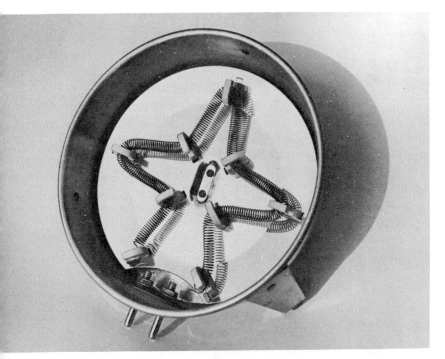

Fig. 1-30. The heating element used in one type of popcorn popper. This one is repairable. However, be sure to measure the length of the replacement wire accurately, in order to get the same operating temperature as before. Other types of poppers may use sealed elements. Again, it must be replaced by the exact duplicate, or the temperature will not be the same.

The open-wire heating element is mounted on ceramic insulation blocks, and power is supplied through a standard plug. If defective, the element is simply replaced.

A similar appliance is the deep-fat fryer. Electrically the two are identical. However, the deep-fat fryers are almost always thermostatically controlled, as are the electric skillets described in the next section.

SKILLETS

The electric skillet is a cooking vessel with a built-in electric heating element which is actually part of the skillet itself, as seen in Fig. 1-31. The thermostat and controls are built into a large plug, or sometimes into the handle.

The control unit is shown in Fig. 1-32. The large aluminum tube between the two electrical contacts is the sensing element for the thermostat, which is riveted to the control unit. Heat from the cooking surface

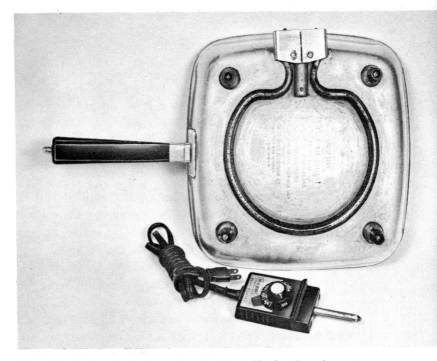

Fig. 1-31. Bottom view of an electric skillet. The heating element is in the aluminum casting, inside the ridge. The thermostatic control unit is in the large plug at the bottom.

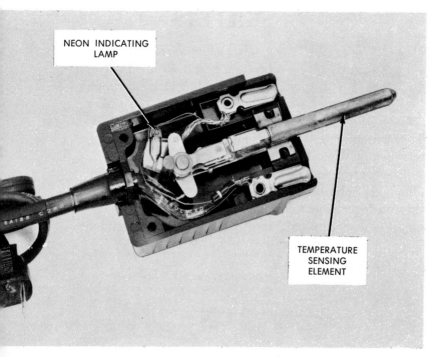

NEON INDICATING LAMP

TEMPERATURE SENSING ELEMENT

Fig. 1-32. A plug-in type thermostatic control unit used with an electric skillet. This is the only repairable part on most skillets, since the heating element is sealed in. Some makes have this control built into the handle. Still, its function remains the same.

travels up the aluminum tubing and is applied to the thermostat, which is adjustable by means of a dial. The tiny neon lamp near the thermostat, when lit, indicates that the heating element is drawing current. It can be seen through the translucent plastic top of the control. Fig. 1-33 shows the typical wiring arrangement used in many electric skillets.

The plug and thermostat are about all that are repairable. The heating elements are so completely sealed into the skillet that it can be completely immersed in water and washed with the dishes. The thermostat control, however, should not be placed under water.

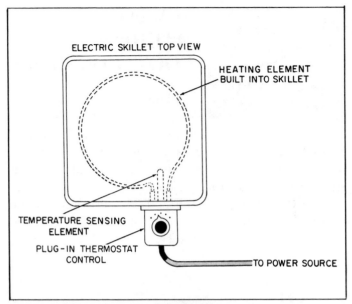

Fig. 1-33. The heating element and thermostat arrangement used on many electric skillets.

Unfortunately, it often is and trouble results. If the heating element opens, the entire skillet must be replaced. Cleaning and adjusting thermostats, and replacing line cords, are about all the servicing you can do, outside of checking the temperature with an oven thermometer.

SEWING-MACHINE FOOT CONTROLS

Many older sewing machines have been electrified by the addition of a small motor controlled by a foot-operated treadle (Fig. 1-34). The control is about as simple as one can get; it consists of a length of resistance wire wound around a ceramic form, with brass taps spaced at intervals (Fig. 1-35). Pressure on the treadle moves the contact arm (at the left) over the taps to regulate the resistance.

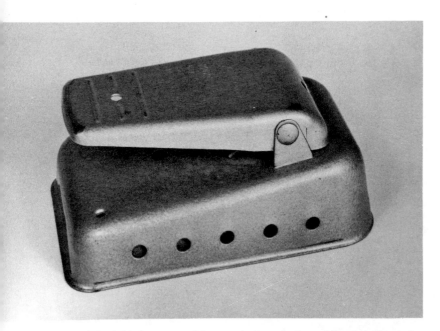

Fig. 1-34. One type of foot control used when older, treadle sewing machines are converted to electrical models. Pressure on the curved treadle moves a contact arm across the resistance element. This action starts, stops, or slows the motor.

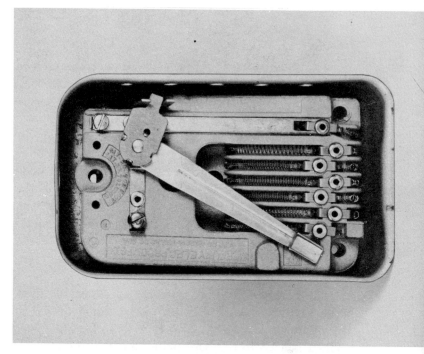

Fig. 1-35. A bottom view of the sewing-machine foot control shown in Fig. 1-34.

All you can do here is see that the resistance wire is not broken and the contact arm is tight. Also watch out for bad insulation on the flexible wire between the terminal and arm. (Incidentally, the control in newer electric sewing machines is electrically identical to this one, differing only in appearance.)

49

BLANKETS

The electric blanket has a flexible heating element sewed right into the material and covering almost the entire area, as seen in Fig. 1-36. A thermostat keeps the temperature constant at the preselected level. In simpler versions, the control is merely a thermostat, pilot light (usually a tiny neon bulb), an on-off switch sometimes incorporated in the thermostat-control knob.

Some blankets have dual controls and two separate heating elements (Fig. 1-37), one for each half of the bed. Thus, the temperature can be individually regulated for each side.

The blanket control box contains an adjustable thermostat with a magnetic contact—a common device in these controls. Fig. 1-38 shows how it works. The lower contact is fixed to the base plate and is surrounded by a small iron washer. Attached to the upper contact arm is a small, cup-shaped magnet (which does *not* make electrical contact in any way).

As the thermostat bends the arm, the magnet gets closer and closer to the fixed contact. Without the magnets, the contact points would come together very slowly until they made contact; this would result in a certain amount of sparking, and the contact would not be firm. By use of the magnets, however, the contacts, when within a certain distance of each other, snap together and make a quick, firm contact. The same action occurs, only in reverse, on a break—the magnets hold the contacts together until the pull of the heating thermostat overcomes the magnetic attraction, and the contacts snap apart.

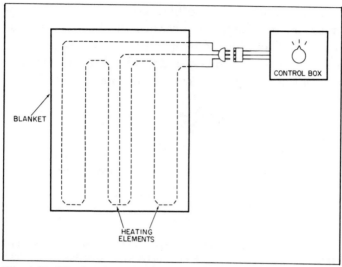

Fig. 1-36. The heating-element arrangement in a single-control electric blanket.

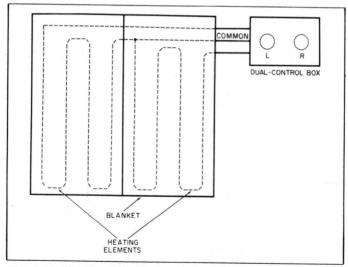

Fig. 1-37. The heating-element arrangement in a dual-control electric blanket. Either side can be controlled independently of the other.

In the simpler electric blankets, the thermostat operates on the difference between the temperature for which it is set and the temperature of the room; there are no sensing elements inside the blanket itself. Hence, should the user put the control unit *under* the electric

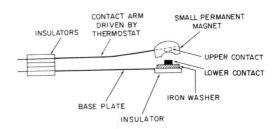

CONTACT ARM DRIVEN BY THERMOSTAT

SMALL PERMANENT MAGNET

INSULATORS

UPPER CONTACT

LOWER CONTACT

IRON WASHER

BASE PLATE

INSULATOR

Fig. 1-38. Construction of magnetic contacts. When these are driven close to each other, the magnetic attraction takes over and snaps them together to provide a firm contact instantaneously.

blanket, the thermostat cannot readily sense room-temperature changes. The control box must be set on a night table or the floor, *never* in the bed. (One poor soul dropped her control box out of bed, and it landed on top of a small night light near the floor. The temperature of the night-light bulb kept the blanket shut off all night!)

In some of the more elaborate blankets using what is called "electronic" control, sensing elements are placed inside the blanket itself. These are connected to the thermostat in the control box, which is slightly more elaborate than the earlier types. By the way, a bypass capacitor of about .05 mfd is connected across the thermostat contacts; if this capacitor shorts out, the blanket will stay on all the time (a common trouble with this type of electric blanket).

The major troubles in blankets are control-box defects, dirty thermostat points, defective capacitors, open elements, and bad line cords or plugs. Open elements are almost never repairable. However, if you can find the break and it is located close to the edge, the seams can be carefully slit open with a razor blade and the element spliced. Be sure to make a good, tight joint; wrap the wire several times and insulate it well with asbestos, tying the whole with thread.

Blankets with internal thermostats can be tested by placing a heating pad under the center, and turning it to various heats while watching the action of the control thermostat. This same procedure is also handy for checking the simpler control boxes. (If it is summer and the room isn't cool enough to lower the temperature to the point where the blanket will turn on, try holding the box in front of an air-conditioner outlet. If none is available, wrap a few ice cubes in a cloth and place under the box.)

HEATING PADS

Heating pads are very similar to electric blankets, but have no control box. The standard pad provides three heats controlled by a selector switch. One resistance element gives a low heat, another a medium heat, and both are connected when high heat is desired. A cable-type wafer, rotary, or push-button switch allows the user to select the desired temperature. Most pads use very small thermostats in series with the heating elements. These are a constant source of trouble in the older models, and even in some of the newer ones. In some makes they can be replaced by ripping a seam at one edge of the pad, opening the cover, and cutting out the defective thermostat. The repair procedure is the same as for electric blankets; make a tight, well-insulated joint in order to prevent a shock hazard to the user.

FANS

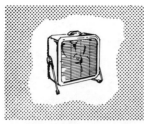

Fig. 1-39 shows a typical small fan with the guard removed. Two nuts hold the motor to the back half of the guard, and the blades are held on by a setscrew. After the blades are removed, the motor can be disassembled by taking off the other two nuts and prying the two halves apart, as in Fig. 1-40. When reassembling, put the two halves of the shell back together (being sure they are seated as before), spin the fan by hand making sure it turns freely, then apply power. With the motor running, tap the housing firmly with a plastic hammer or the handle of a large

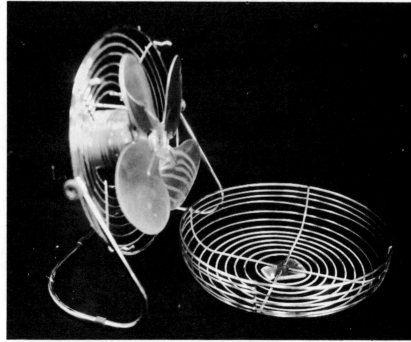

Fig. 1-39. A small electric fan with the guard removed.

Fig. 1-40. The fan in Fig. 1-39 disassembled. A setscrew holds the
blade on.

screwdriver; the jar will cause the captive ball bearings
to line up with the shaft. Tighten the nuts firmly and
the job is done.

Blades can get out of balance and cause vibration.
Fasten the fan motor firmly to something heavy enough
to hold it. Construct some kind of "indicator" so the
tip of each blade just touches it. Spin the blades by
hand, and bend any misaligned blades back into line.
Also watch the blades from the side to detect any with
too much pitch, which can also cause vibration.

Other than defective switches and line cords, there's
little else to give trouble in fans. Motors rarely fail, even
when improperly cared for. For the occasional motor
trouble you might experience, refer to Chapter 4.

CAN OPENERS

The electric can opener (Fig. 1-41) is mechanically similar to the hand-operated model. Fig. 1-42, a close-up of its cutting mechanism, verifies this similarity. A can is hooked under the toothed wheel at the lower center, and the lever is pushed down until flush with the top of the case, causing a stud on the lever to close the switch and start the motor. The actual cutting is done by the cutting wheel just above the

Fig. 1-41. A combination electric can opener and knife sharpener. Knives are sharpened by holding them against the small grinding wheel, accessible through the slot in the chrome-plated cover at the back of machine.

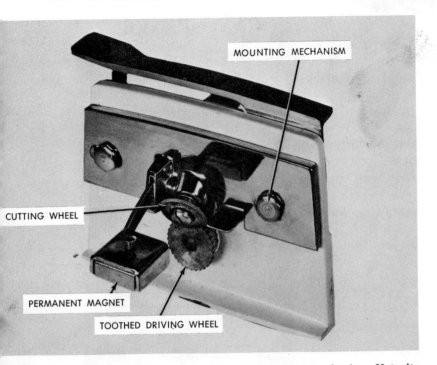

MOUNTING MECHANISM

CUTTING WHEEL

PERMANENT MAGNET

TOOTHED DRIVING WHEEL

Fig. 1-42. Close-up view of the can-opener mechanism. Note its similarity to hand-operated models. The toothed wheel at the lower center drives the rim of the can; the small round wheel above is the cutting blade.

toothed driving wheel. A permanent magnet attached to a small arm pulls the lid of the can off after it is cut free. Cutting tension is regulated by the spring-loaded screw marked "Keep Screw Tight" at the right. If cleaning or resharpening is necessary, the cutting assembly can be removed by taking out this screw and another one just like it on the left side.

Fig. 1-43 shows a close-up of the shaded-pole motor used (see later chapter on motors). It has no brushes, being similar to a phonograph motor. Note the gearing by which the motor drives the can opener and the tiny grinding wheel at the left. This model is a dual-purpose

Fig. 1-43. Shaded-pole motor used in the electric can opener of
Fig. 1-41. This type is almost an exact duplicate of the familiar
phonograph motor, only a little heavier. No brushes are used.
Lubrication is about the only servicing needed.

one that also serves as a knife sharpener. The slots for
the knife blade can be seen at the back of the housing
in Fig. 1-41. The small square block on the free end of
the grinding-wheel shaft is a nylon bushing that fits
into a recess in the chromium-plated cover. The cover
can be slipped off, without disassembling the whole
machine, by removing the three Phillips screws holding it.

To disassemble this machine, take out the Phillips
screws around the front of the housing. The upper part
of the housing can then be lifted off, exposing the motor
and gears. The cutter-drive gear housing is permanently

riveted in place. If absolutely necessary, the ends of these rivets could be ground off and the cover removed for replacement of gears. Then the cover could be re-fastened by drilling out the rivets and installing small bolts and nuts.

Except for the motor (and the cord and plug, of course), electric can openers are strictly mechanical devices. Most troubles, therefore, will be due to dulled cutting edges, worn gears, etc., which may need replacement from time to time. Cleaning and lubrication is needed at least twice a year. If motor troubles are suspected, refer to the later chapter on this subject.

ROTISSERIES

The rotisserie (Fig. 1-44) is a fairly new addition to the appliance field. Briefly, it consists of a heating element, and a spit rotated by a small electric motor. The heating element (not seen in Fig. 1-44 because it is at the top of the cabinet) is fairly large and is sealed like those in electric ranges. It is in the shape of a loop and covers the whole top of the cabinet.

This particular model can be used for rotary broiling

Fig. 1-44. Front view of a typical rotisserie, used for rotary broiling. A motor rotates the spit at a constant speed to provide even cooking. The door is made of oven glass. If it must be replaced, use the same heat-resistant type.

of meats or, without the spit, for ordinary broiling and baking. All of the works are enclosed in the left side of the cabinet. The lower knob is the thermostat, and the three push-button switches at the top allow the user to select "Broil," "Rotisserie," or "Outlet." (The last is for the appliance outlet at the bottom of the panel.)

A small motor is mounted on the left panel, with a splined socket for the spit. To disassemble, remove the Phillips screws around the edges of the cabinet and lift off the top and sides, exposing the motor and thermostat. The temperature settings of the heating element can be checked by placing an oven thermometer inside the cabinet, at about the level of the spit. (Be sure to close the door.)

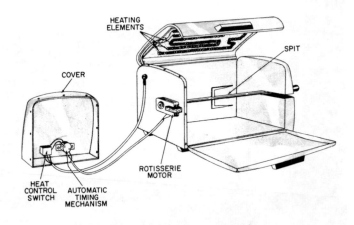

Fig. 1-45. Location of components in one type of rotisserie.

Some rotisseries are equipped with a timer to permit cooking for a predetermined length of time. Fig. 1-45 shows a rotisserie using such a timer. The side cover of the unit has been removed to illustrate the positions of the various components. Inside the end cover you can see the heat-control switch at the left; the automatic timing mechanism is located to the right. Both are set by the control knobs located on the outside cover. The heating element is mounted underneath the lid as shown, and may be either an exposed or a sealed unit. A small motor, mounted on the side, drives the spit.

There isn't too much that will need servicing on a rotisserie. You will encounter defective line cords, heating elements, switches, and occasionally some motor trouble. Incidentally, if the motor requires lubrication, be sure to use only silicone grease, which can withstand the high temperatures.

CHAPTER 2

LINE CORDS PLUGS and ATTACHMENTS

By far the most common service job on appliances is replacement of line cords and plugs. Constant flexing, aging, and abuse cause them to wear out rapidly.

TYPES OF CORDS USED

Each appliance uses a line cord selected for its particular service. Small appliances employ the common zip cord used on TV sets and radios. Others use a slightly heavier jacketed wire; the heaviest of all is the asbestos-insulated wire for electric irons and heaters. No matter what the type, though, it must be flexible. So from now on, whenever any line cord is mentioned, remember that it is *always* stranded wire. (The only solid wires used in appliances are in heating elements and similar applications.)

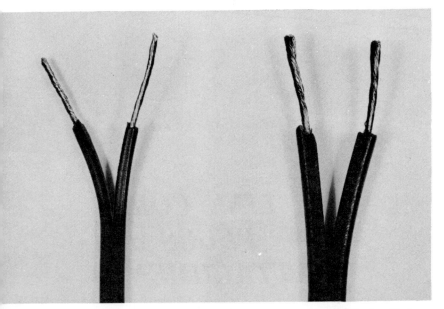

Fig. 2-1. Zip cord, more correctly known as POSJ (an Underwriter's Code designation), is used for many appliances. The No.
18 gauge at the left is the more common; it is employed on appliances requiring relatively small loads. At the right is a section
of No. 16 gauge for heavier-duty applications. Notice the "groove"
down the center, for easy separation of the conductors.

POSJ Cord

POSJ is the Underwriter's Code classification for zip
cord. It is rubber- or plastic-insulated (Fig. 2-1) and
has a groove down the center for easy separation—
hence the name, zip cord. Each conductor is wrapped
with a fiber "lay" inside the insulation. Zip, or POSJ,
cord is available in sizes from No. 18 (the smallest) up
to about No. 10.

SV Cord

SV cord is a jacketed cable consisting of two rubber-
insulated wires over a fiber lay, with an additional fiber

Fig. 2-2. SV cord is a jacketed cable used for heavy-duty service. It consists of two stranded conductors, each one insulated with rubber. A fiber "filler" is used between the wires, and a rubber or plastic jacket covers the entire assembly.

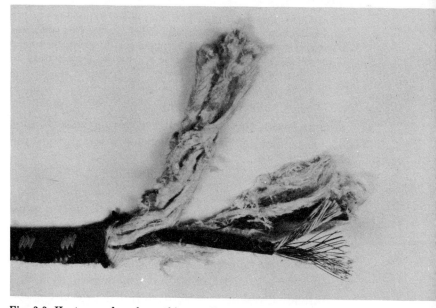

Fig. 2-3. Heater cord such as this usually employs stranded conductors of about No. 14 or 12 gauge. These are insulated with rubber and wrapped with asbestos fibers. The entire assembly is then covered with a stout braided jacket.

67

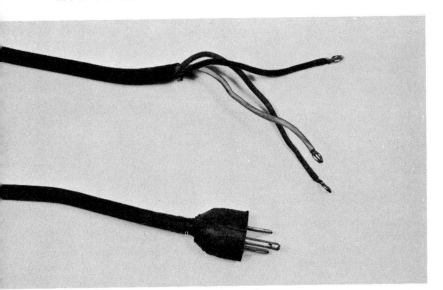

Fig. 2-4. This three-wire cable is similar to the SV cord in Fig. 2-2, but has an extra conductor (usually coded green). This conductor is connected to the frame of the appliance, in order to ground it for safety and thereby eliminate a possible shock hazard to the user.

filler between them. The outer covering consists of a heavy rubber or plastic jacket for added protection (Fig. 2-2).

Heater Cord

Heater cord should always be used on electric irons, waffle irons, and any other appliance whose heating elements draw more than 500 watts. (An electric iron consumes one kilowatt, as do waffle irons and grilles.) Each wire has a fiber wrap and rubber insulation, and is individually wrapped with stranded asbestos fibers. An extra fiber or asbestos filler is placed around both wires, and the outer covering is a tightly-woven braided jacket (Fig. 2-3).

Three-Wire Cable

Three-wire cable is a rubber-jacketed wire often used on drills and similar tools. It is like the SV cord, but has an additional wire which is used as a grounding conductor (Fig. 2-4). This third wire, generally coded green, is fastened to the frame of the appliance; and the other end goes to a third prong on a special line plug, or to a pigtail coming out of the cable just above the plug. (The pigtail should be connected to a good ground.) Incidentally, this type of cord can be installed on any electrical appliance. It should always be employed where the user may have to stand on damp or conductive material such as cement floors, earth, etc.

WIRE SIZES

Line cords must be able to carry the normal current without heating up and causing a loss of power. Table 2-1 shows the current-carrying capacity of standard

Table 2-1. Capacity of flexible cord (in amperes).

Size AWG	Rubber Types PO, C, PD, P, PW, K, E, EO Thermoplastic Type ET	Rubber Types S, SO, SRD, SJ, SJO, SV, SP Thermoplastic Types ST, SRDT, SJT, SVT, SPT	Types AFS, AFSJ, HC, HPD, HSJ, HS, HPN	Types AVPO, AVPD	Cotton Types CFC* CFPO* CFPD* Asbestos Types AFC* AFPO* AFPD*
18	5	7	10	17	6
17	..	..	12	..	..
16	7	10	15	22	8
15	..	..	17	..	..
14	15	15	20	28	17
12	20	20	30	36	23
10	25	25	35	47	28
8	35	35	..	..	..
6	45	45	..	..	..
4	60	60	..	..	..
2	80	..	..	..	..

* These types are used almost exclusively in fixtures where they are exposed to high temperatures and ampere ratings are assigned accordingly.

Table 2-2. Types of flexible cable.

Trade Name	Type Letter	Size AWG	No. of Conductors	Insulation	Outer Covering	Use
Asbestos-Covered Heat-Resistant Cord	AFC	18-10	2 or 3	Impregnated Asbestos	None	Pendant, Dry Places, Not Hard Usage
	AFPO		2		Cotton, Rayon or Saturated Asbestos	
	AFPD		2 or 3			
Cotton-Covered Heat-Resistant Cord	CFC	18-10	2 or 3	Impregnated Cotton	None	Pendant, Dry Places, Not Hard Usage
	CFPO		2		Cotton or Rayon	
	CFPD		2 or 3			
All Rubber Parallel Cord	SP-1	18	2	Rubber		Pendant or Portable, Damp Places, Not Hard Usage
	SP-2	18-16	2	Rubber	Rubber	Refrigerators or Room Air Conditioners
	SP-3	18-12		Rubber	Rubber	Pendant or Portable, Damp Places, Hard Usage
All Plastic Parallel Cord	SPT-1	18	2	Thermoplastic		Refrigerators or Room Air Conditioners
	SPT-2	18-16	2	Thermoplastic	Thermoplastic	Pendant or Portable, Dry Places, Not Hard Usage
	SPT-3	18-12		Thermoplastic	Thermoplastic	Pendant or Portable, Dry Places, Not Hard Usage
Lamp Cord	C	18-10	2 or more	Rubber	None	Pendant or Portable, Dry Places, Not Hard Usage
Twisted Portable Cord	PD	18-10	2 or more	Rubber	Cotton or Rayon	Hard Usage
Reinforced Cord	P-1	18	2 or more	Rubber	Cotton over Rubber Filler	Pendant or Portable, Dry Places, Not Hard Usage
	P-2	18-16				Pendant or Portable, Dry Places, Not Hard Usage
	P	18-10				Hard Usage
Moisture-Proof Reinforced Cord	PW-1	18	2 or more	Rubber	Cotton, Moisture-Resistant Finish over Rubber Filler	Pendant or Portable, Damp Places, Hard Usage
	PW-2	18-16				Hard Usage
	PW	18-10				Hard Usage

Table 2-1. The current-carrying capacity

Type of Cord	Designation	Size (AWG)	No. of Conductors	Insulation	Outer Covering	Use
Braided Heavy Duty Cord	K	18-10	2 or more	Rubber	Two Cotton, Moisture-Resistant Finish	Pendant or Portable, Damp Places, Hard Usage
Vacuum Cleaner Cord	SV	18	2	Rubber	Rubber	Pendant or Portable, Damp Places, Not Hard Usage
	SVT			Thermoplastic	Thermoplastic	
Junior Hard Service Cord	SJ	18-16	2, 3, or 4	Rubber	Rubber	Pendant or Portable, Damp Places, Hard Usage
	SJO			Rubber	Oil Resistant Compound	
	SJT			Thermoplastic or Rubber	Thermoplastic	
Hard Service Cord	S	18-10	2 or more	Rubber	Rubber	Pendant or Portable, Damp Places, Extra Hard Usage
	SO			Rubber	Oil Resistant Compound	
	ST			Thermoplastic or Rubber	Thermoplastic	
Rubber-Jacketed Heat-Resistant Cord	AFSJ	18-16	2 or 3	Impregnated Asbestos	Rubber	Damp Places, Portable Heaters
	AFS	18-16-14				
Heater Cord	HC	18-12	2, 3, or 4	Rubber & Asbestos	None	Dry Places, Portable Heaters
	HPD			Rubber & Asbestos	Cotton or Rayon	
Rubber Jacketed Heater Cord	HSJ	18-16	2, 3, or 4	Rubber & Asbestos	Cotton and Rubber	Damp Places, Portable Heaters
Jacketed Heater Cord	HS	14-12	2, 3, or 4	Rubber & Asbestos	Cotton and Rubber or Neoprene	Damp Places, Portable Heaters
All-Neoprene Heater Cord	HPN	18-16	2	Neoprene	Neoprene	Damp Places, Portable Heaters
Heat & Moisture-Resistant Cord	AVPO	18-10	2	Asbestos and Var. Cam.	Asbestos, Flame-Resistant Moisture Resistant	Pendant or Portable, Damp Places, Not Hard Usage
	AVPD		2 or 3			

of various standard sizes of wire.

wire sizes. Somewhere on every appliance is a rating plate showing the total wattage required. From $W = EI$ we get $I = W \div E$, from which we can find the current. This need not be a precise figure. For example, an appliance drawing 200 watts at 110 volts would have a current of about 2 amperes. Note that any of the types of No. 18 wire listed in Table 2-1 will handle this current with an adequate safety factor. Remember, these wires are stranded and some of the strands will eventually break from the continual flexing. If the wire is large enough, it will still have enough strands left to hold up for quite a while; but wire that is too small will overheat and present a definite fire hazard. In making any electrical repairs—especially appliance repairs—the utmost in safety should be your major objective; the appliances will be used by women and children, most of whom are a little short on knowledge of electricity and safety precautions.

PLUGS

Quite a few types of plugs are used on appliances— some for connecting to the power source, and others for connection to the appliance itself. Almost all original-

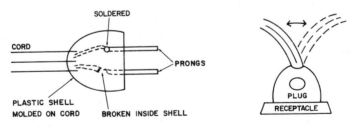

(A) Where break usually occurs.   (B) Method of checking.

Fig. 2-5. Power cords often cause trouble by opening or shorting at the plug.

Fig. 2-6. Replacement plugs are available in a variety of types. Some typical examples are shown above.

equipment cords are terminated in a molded plastic plug; the small one on a TV line cord is a good example (Fig. 2-5).

The most frequent trouble is a broken wire inside the plug, as shown in Fig. 2-5A. This is due to constant flexing of the wire, and can be hard to find unless you're watching for it. Whenever repairing *any* appliance using such a plug, check by bending the wire back and forth (Fig. 2-5B) with the appliance turned on, and watch for signs of intermittent contact. If trouble shows up, clip off the plug and replace it.

There are several choices here: probably the best for all-round replacement is the rubber-shell type with removable prongs. A group of appliance replacement plugs is shown in Fig. 2-6. At the left is a plastic plug; the end of the wire is slipped into the lower part and the prongs pushed together. Spikes penetrate the insulation, and the shell holds it in place. The two in the center are connected by attaching the wires to screws. At the right is a molded rubber plug with an insert; it is very durable and is recommended for most replacement work because it will carry any of the standard household appliances, even 1-kilowatt electric irons.

CHECKING LINE CORDS FOR WEAR AND AGING

Whenever any electrical appliance is checked, the line cord should be inspected very carefully. Worn or aged insulation can create a fire hazard.

Years ago, line cords were made of reclaimed rubber or the early synthetics, and they understandably weren't too good! These cords caused more than their share of trouble when placed near a window, because direct sunlight played havoc with them. In later years, improved synthetics have made the line cords quite durable—but watch out for the older ones!

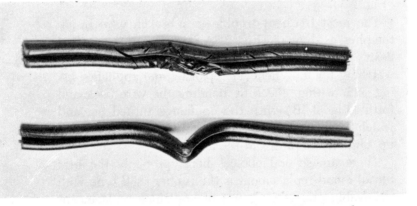

Fig. 2-7. Line cords can become dangerous. The ones above are often referred to as "The Fireman's Friend," and when in this condition should be replaced rather than repaired.

The quickest insulation test is to bend the cord sharply between the fingers. If the surface shows tiny cracks or it crumbles off entirely (Fig. 2-7), replace the cord. Look for most troubles to occur at the ends, where the greatest amount of flexing occurs. At times the cord will be worn only at the ends. If it won't make the cord too short, clip out the bad parts and replace the plug. Check first, though, or you may get into trouble! I cut off about six inches of a line cord one day, only to receive a severe tongue lashing the next! It seems the cord "had been" just long enough to put the mixer where the lady wanted it. She kept after me until I installed a new cord.

CORD ATTACHMENTS AND STRAIN RELIEFS

At the point where the line cord goes into the appliance, there should always be a firm anchorage to keep any strain off the electrical connections. Devices used for this purpose are called *strain reliefs*, and several are shown in Fig. 2-8. In Fig. 2-8A the power cord is passed through a rubber grommet to provide further protection, or a clamp like that shown in Fig. 2-8B may be used. Fig. 2-8C shows a plastic strain-relief device in two sections, one for each side of the cord. When assembled, it is held tightly in a pair of pliers and forced into the hole in the chassis. The kink in the center holds the line cord securely, and the outside notches snap behind the lip of the hole to keep the entire assembly in place. Always put a strain relief on an appliance if it has none, and be sure it holds the wire firmly, in order to keep any strain from being placed on the electrical connections.

If the body of the appliance normally gets very hot (such as a waffle iron), don't use soft rubber grommets or anything that would be damaged by heat. Instead, use the hard fiber grommets made especially for the purpose.

Two appliances whose line cords require special protection, because of the high heat and frequent move-

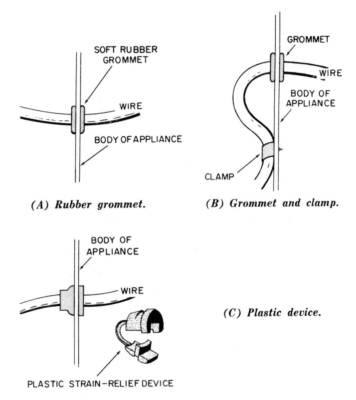

(A) Rubber grommet.

(B) Grommet and clamp.

(C) Plastic device.

Fig. 2-8. Examples of various strain-relieving methods.

ment to which they are subjected, are irons and waffle irons. An iron, of course, needs more attention, since its cord is constantly being pulled, twisted, and bent during use. This was one of the big reasons why the detachable plug was eliminated in favor of a permanently attached cord.

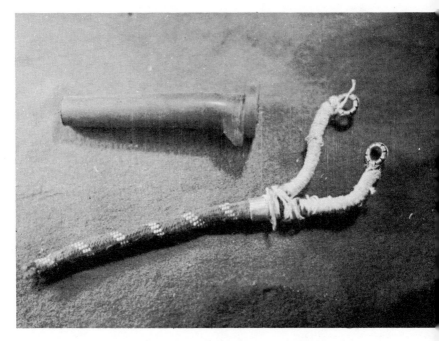

Fig. 2-9. An iron cord ready for installation. Notice the small metal clamp where the wires divide; this is used to keep the strain off the electrical connections. The soft rubber sleeve shown in the photo prevents the cord from being bent and kinked too sharply.

Fig. 2-9 shows a typical cord for an iron. The tapered rubber sleeve on the end keeps the wire from being bent too sharply, and eases the strain due to the continual pulling and twisting. When repairing iron cords, be sure to replace this sleeve if missing or worn.

Waffle irons and similar appliances have two heating elements, one on the lid and one on the bottom. The interconnecting wires are wrapped tightly in asbestos and enclosed in a spiral spring-like protector, shown in Fig. 2-10 (rubber wouldn't do at all because of the excessive heat). Check the wiring inside these appliances every time they are serviced, to make sure there are no worn places to cause a short circuit.

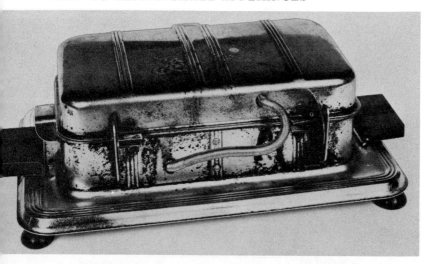

Fig. 2-10. The spiral device shown between the two halves of this waffle iron isn't a spring, but a flexible steel protector surrounding the interconnecting leads. The leads themselves are made of stranded copper to hold up under the constant flexing and heat, and are heavily wrapped with asbestos.

APPLIANCE CONNECTORS

Heavy-duty detachable appliance connectors, although no longer used on irons, are used extensively with waffle irons, grilles, toasters, coffee makers, and numerous other appliances.

These plugs are alike except in size. Fig. 2-11 shows one disassembled. The very heavy contacts allow the plug to carry up to a kilowatt without overheating, and the channels or grooves in the shell provide an automatic strain relief for the line cord. When reassembling these plugs, be sure to dress the wire neatly down in the grooves; otherwise the shell may be broken when the screws are tightened.

Almost all connectors provide line-cord protection, such as the spring shown or a rubber sleeve. It should

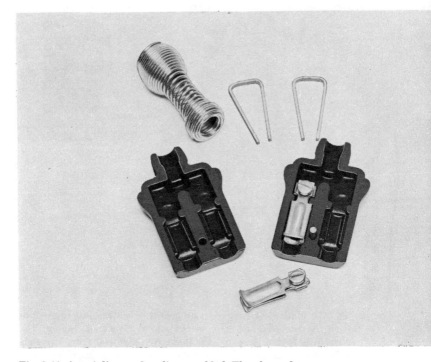

Fig. 2-11. An appliance plug disassembled. The channels or grooves inside the shell serve as strain reliefs to hold the wire tightly, should the user make a practice of disconnecting the plug by pulling it out by the cord. The actual contacts are also held in grooves. A spiral spring at the rear of the plug prevents the cord from being bent too sharply; the entire unit is held together by two small machine screws.

be in place before reassembling the plug. (Slip it over the wire *first*, and then put the plug together.)

There is a special way of preparing the cord for attachment to this type of plug. First, carefully slit the outer jacket about two inches from the end, and clip it off. Separate the wires and remove about three-fourths inch of insulation from the ends (Fig. 2-12). Rewrap the asbestos around each wire, up to the exposed part. Now take a spool of common fine thread and wrap it tightly around each wire. The thread wrap-

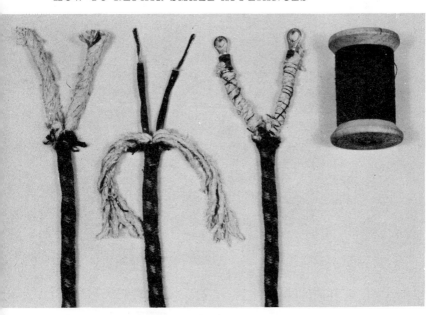

Fig. 2-12. Method of preparing an asbestos heater cord for installation. At the left, the wire is cut and ready for stripping. The asbestos is folded back and the insulation stripped from the ends of the wires (center). At the right, the asbestos fibers are held in place by wrapping thread around them, and circular lugs are attached to the ends of the wires.

ping keeps the asbestos in place and thus makes the wire much easier to handle.

Attach lugs to the ends of the wires (Fig. 2-13), if the plug is big enough to hold them. If not, tin the ends well and loop each one to fit the connecting screw. Tighten these screws securely, for they will be carrying a heavy current; if loose, they will arc and develop a high resistance, in addition to overheating. (Motto in all work like this: a clean, tight connection is a cool one!)

If the cord is being attached to an iron, use connecting lugs like the type in Fig. 2-13. Notice that no solder is used in these lugs, because the temperature of the

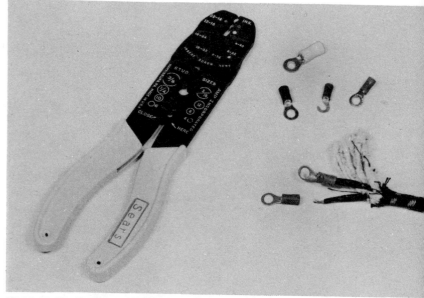

Fig. 2-13. Method of connecting special lugs for heavy-duty operation, such as irons and other devices using heating elements that require a large current. These lugs require no solder; the stripped wire is slipped into the lug and secured by the use of a crimping tool. The tool is applied twice—once where the bare wire touches the lug, and once over the insulation. Different styles are available.

connections is ordinarily above the melting point of solder. This type of lug should be crimped to both the wire and the insulation, and held tightly by the terminal nuts.

FASTENERS AND WIRE NUTS

The common terminal screw is used for almost all electrical connections in appliances. However, where it is necessary to fasten wires to wires without any terminals (a typical example is the motor leads of a mixer), a special fastener called a wire nut is used. These are

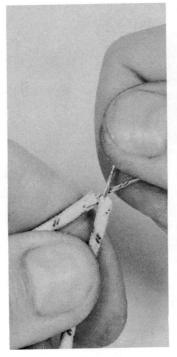 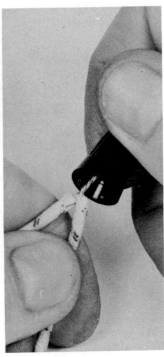

(A) Prepared splice.   (B) Wire nut installed.

Fig. 2-14. Method of using a wire nut.

made of cone-shaped plastic or ceramic, with a threaded hole in the center.

The method of using this device is illustrated in Fig. 2-14. The insulation is stripped from the ends of the wires to be joined, and the wires are twisted together as shown in Fig. 2-14A. The wire nut is then screwed tightly onto the connection until it covers the insulation (Fig. 2-14B). The ends of the wires should not be stripped back too far—about three-fourths of an inch or so is usually enough. The wire nut should screw onto the connection far enough so that no bare wires will be left exposed when the connection is completed. (Some

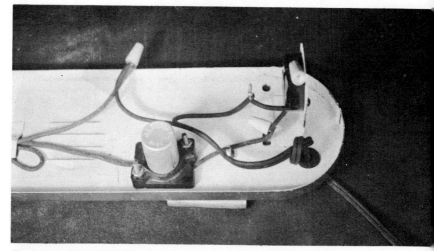

Fig. 2-15. Wire-nuts such as these are often used to secure a splice. The two wires to be joined are twisted together as shown and the wire-nut screwed over the connection, holding it securely.

versions use a small conical brass spring instead of the molded threads.) Fig. 2-15 shows wire nuts used in a lighting fixture.

CHAPTER 3

HEATING ELEMENTS and THERMOSTATS

A lot of home appliances are basically nothing more than heating elements. Electric irons, grilles, toasters, waffle irons, heating pads, and blankets are some examples. A heating element is fundamentally an electrical conductor of suitable size connected directly across the AC line. The first heating elements were spiral types resembling coil springs suspended between insulating holders. Early electric "hot plates" consisted of a grooved ceramic material (called a "brick") into which a spiral heating element (Fig. 3-1) was placed.

Its disadvantages were obvious; since the element glowed red hot in open air, this brought on rapid oxidation, and the exposed wire presented a constant shock hazard. Later types use the completely sealed element

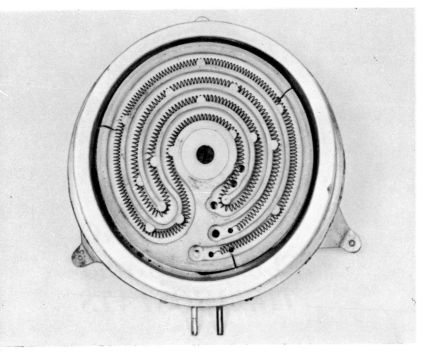

Fig. 3-1. An older-type "hot plate" with an exposed heating element mounted within the circular recess of a ceramic insulator (often referred to as a "brick").

shown in Fig. 3-2. It is made of flat ribbon wire with a heat-resistant insulation of ceramic, mica, etc., and enclosed in a solid metal cover. This basic element is used in many appliances today, with variations in shape to suit the type of appliance. If the element is open, it cannot be repaired because of its sealed construction, but must be replaced with the exact duplicate in size, shape, and rating.

CONTROLLING THE HEAT

The amount of heat is controlled automatically in such devices by means of a thermostat (literally, "con-

Fig. 3-2. A "hot plate" employing sealed elements. The elements themselves are enclosed in a solid ceramic brick which is sealed into a metal housing. The unit at the bottom center is a switch that permits selection of various degrees of heat.

stant heat"), which is a switch that automatically turns power to the element on and off to keep its temperature stable within just a few degrees.

The heart of all thermostats is a bimetal blade (Fig. 3-3), a strip of metal made from two unlike alloys, one with a high rate of expansion when heated, and the other with a low rate. When heated (Fig. 3-3A), the high-expansion metal is "held" by the one with a low rate, and the combination of forces causes the blade to bend, as shown in Fig. 3-3B. When the heat is removed, the blade returns to its normally straight position.

This action can be used to control the heat from an electric heater. This is done by placing the bimetal blade where the heat from the main heating element will raise its temperature. When the heat rises above a predetermined level (fixed by the design of the thermostat blade), the blade bends, opening the contact; and the heating element cools off. When the temperature of the blade (and apparatus) drops to a lower limit, the blade straightens out once more, closing the contact; and the heating element goes on again. This process is repeated constantly while the appliance is on.

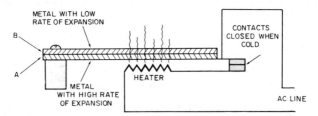

(A) Blade cool, beginning to heat up.

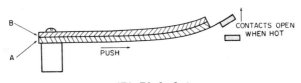

(B) Blade hot.

Fig. 3-3. Thermostatic action of a bimetal blade. Metal "A" has a high rate of expansion with heat, and metal "B" a low expansion rate.

By altering the proportion and alloy of the two metals in the blade, thermostats can be designed to give almost any desired temperature control. All thermostats have an upper limit (the temperature at which the contacts open) and a lower limit (the temperature at which

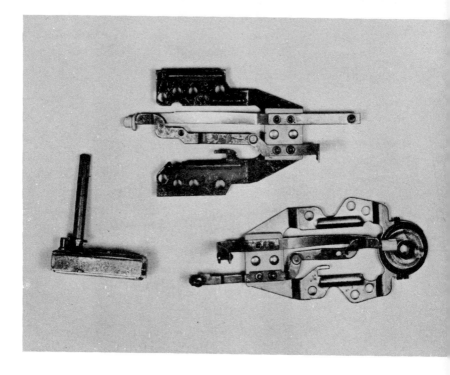

Fig. 3-4. Typical thermostats used with electric irons. Although they come in many sizes and shapes, their function remains the same—to control the amount of heat.

they close). In precision applications they can be made so sensitive that the temperature is kept constant to within one degree. Ordinary appliance thermostats do not have to be quite so sensitive.

The thermostats in the more common appliances are almost always adjustable. Fig. 3-4 shows some thermostats used in electric irons. The temperature of the iron is controlled by a screw, which varies the distance between the contact points and thus the amount the temperature must rise to open them. After this temperature is reached, the thermostat keeps the iron at the desired

89

heat (within five to seven degrees). Similar applications are found in all coffee makers, toasters, electric blankets, and other heat-producing appliances. Sometimes the temperature-controlling action of the thermostat is combined to provide a timing action. For instance, in some toasters a small heating element is wound around the thermostat blade. The current drawn by the main heating element flows through this smaller element and heats the blade. The auxiliary element is of such a size that it causes the blade to warp and open the contacts within a preset number of minutes or seconds. This device is used to make toast just the right shade or to boil coffee for so many minutes, and in many other applications requiring timed heat.

TESTING AND REPAIRING
HEATING ELEMENTS

One way to check a heating element is by a simple continuity test with an ohmmeter (a tester that measures the electrical resistance of conductors). The second and more accurate test is to measure the wattage drawn by the element. Wattmeters are available in several versions. The one in Fig. 3-5 is a complete appliance tester containing a three-range wattmeter and AC voltmeter, plus facilities for making a continuity test. Push buttons permit selection of two auxiliary wattage ranges—100 watts and 20 watts—for checking low-drain appliances. (Incidentally, if special cables are added to the triple binding posts on the lower part of the instrument panel, even electric ranges can be checked.)

The proper safe wattage is always given on the "Underwriter's" label, usually fastened to the appliance in some inconspicuous place. If this label has been removed, you'll have to guess at the wattage; but from experience you should be able to make a close enough

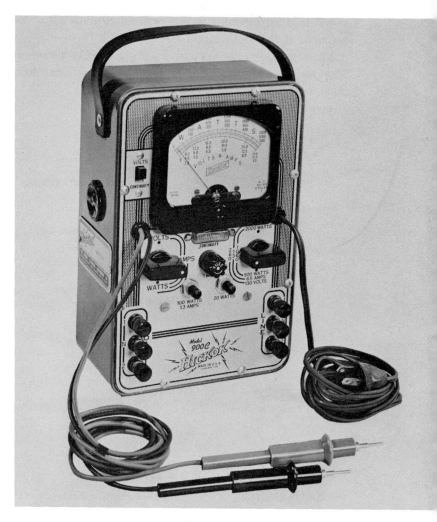

(Courtesy Hickok Electrical Instrument Co.)

Fig. 3-5. An instrument used for testing appliances.

estimate. For instance, almost all late-model electric irons draw approximately one kilowatt.

If a sealed heating element is open, there isn't much else you can do but replace it, and always with an exact duplicate because of space problems. Now and then you'll find an element with open leads, and it can be repaired if the right method is followed.

Most elements use very heavy copper wire, known as "copper rope," to carry the heavy currents without loss.

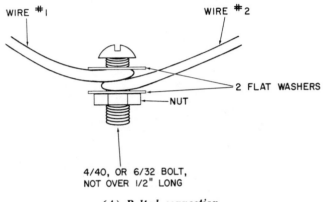

WIRE #1 WIRE #2

2 FLAT WASHERS

NUT

4/40, OR 6/32 BOLT,
NOT OVER 1/2" LONG

(A) Bolted connection.

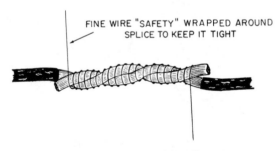

FINE WIRE "SAFETY" WRAPPED AROUND
SPLICE TO KEEP IT TIGHT

(B) Safety-wrapped splice.

Fig. 3-6. Two methods of splicing a wire carrying heavy current.

In some applications, small ceramic beads are used as insulation; others use a wrapping of asbestos. Be sure to replace worn or broken insulation in order to prevent a shock or fire hazard.

Splicing wires in high-current circuits can be difficult. The joint must be able to carry the same current as the original wire; if loose or dirty, it will immediately overheat and burn out. It isn't possible to solder the joints in these wires, especially on large heating elements, because the wiring often runs above the melting point of ordinary solder. So, unless you use silver solder, the best way is to wrap the ends of the wire around a small bolt and nut between two flat washers (Fig. 3-6A), tightening the whole thing to hold the wires firmly in place and thus keep the joint resistance low. An alternative method, if there is enough original lead left, is to make a tightly twisted joint, winding at least three turns of wire around each other. This can be "safetied" by wrapping it with several turns of fine wire pulled very tight (Fig. 3-6B). Always clean the ends of the wires thoroughly so the joint will have the lowest possible resistance. If there is enough room at the bottom of the appliance, a small ceramic wire nut can be used.

When a splice must be insulated, there is a special tape available for this purpose made of *Fiberglas*. Never use friction or plastic tape—it wouldn't last five minutes under the terrific heat! If no *Fiberglas* tape is on hand, discarded asbestos insulation from a wire can be used. Wrap it tightly around the joint and tie it in place with long fibers of asbestos, which can usually be unwound from a scrap of wire in three- or four-inch lengths.

CHAPTER 4

SMALL ELECTRIC MOTORS

Next to heating elements, small electric motors are the most common devices used in home appliances. These are of two major types: the synchronous and the brush type. Synchronous motors are not usually used in applications calling for fairly large amounts of power, and never where the speed must be controlled. You'll find them in clocks, for example. Brush-commutator types, on the other hand, have a much higher torque and are used where the speed must be varied, such as in sewing machines, mixers, etc.

Synchronous motors like the one in Fig. 4-1 are universally used in phonographs and record changers (where a steady speed is essential). Because of their low power requirements, they seldom give any trouble electrically; the biggest difficulty will be lack of lubrication in the bearings. A thorough cleaning and relubrication will solve most service problems.

Brush-type motors offer more chances for trouble, mainly from worn brushes and defective armatures. The basic electrical circuit for this type of motor is shown in Fig. 4-2. Note in Fig. 4-2A that the armature

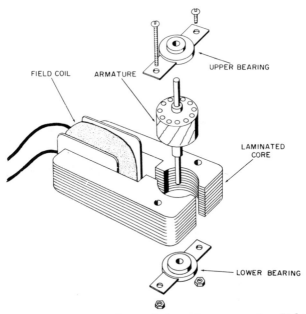

Fig. 4-1. Construction of a typical synchronous motor. It has no brushes or commutator, and is employed where a constant speed and relatively little power is needed.

is connected between the two field coils. This connection has been adopted by almost all manufacturers of late; in the older types the fields and motor were connected separately, as in Fig. 4-2B. By placing the armature and brushes between the two field coils as shown in Fig. 4-2A, excessive brush noise from the motor is reduced. Operation is the same with either connection. (In fact, older motors can be reconnected this way if you wish.)

It might be a good idea here to run over the theory of operation of brush motors. They have two field coils mounted on the motor frame, as seen in Fig. 4-3. Suspended inside this frame is the rotor or armature. The armature consists of a laminated metal structure with coils of copper wire wound in the slots. The ends of each armature coil are connected to a pair of commutator segments (shown by the dotted lines), and carbon brushes make contact with them.

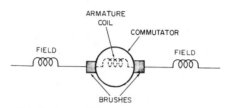

(A) Coil on either side of armature.

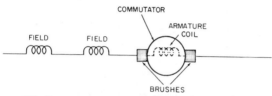

(B) Both coils on same side of armature.

Fig. 4-2. Two methods of connecting the field coils in an electric motor.

At any given instant, the two field coils and one of the coils on the armature are in series across the AC line. Current flows through the coils and sets up a magnetic field inside the motor, between the frame and armature. Because of the way the coils are connected, the magnetic field is always unbalanced—that is, it exerts a force against both the frame and the armature. The armature is the only part free to move; so it turns in an effort to balance the magnetic fields. As it does, the armature coil causing the unbalance is disconnected (before it has a chance to balance) and another is reconnected in its place, causing still more unbalance. This process is repeated, keeping the armature rotating until the current is disconnected. The motor speed is determined by the frequency of the applied voltage and the number of coils on the armature.

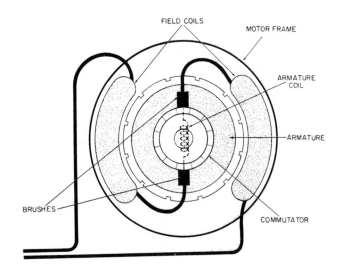

Fig. 4-3. Internal construction of a small motor. The electrical path between the brushes is completed through a coil in the armature.

TROUBLES IN BRUSH MOTORS

You'll find two kinds of troubles in brush motors: they won't run fast enough, or they won't run at all. The first trouble is almost always due to a dry bearing in the armature. Once in awhile, a defective armature will cause this condition; but when it does, you'll know it! We'll find out why in a moment.

To check a completely dead motor, the best way is to use an ohmmeter to make a quick continuity test, to determine if there are any breaks in the line cord, field coils, and brushes. You should get a reading of only a few ohms across the line-plug terminals with the motor switch on (disconnected from the power source, of course). The exact amount of resistance will depend on the size of wire used in the motor, but your main concern at this point is whether or not a reading can be obtained. A very high reading (several thousand ohms) indicates a partially open circuit, more often than not because of faulty brushes.

Brush Troubles

Brushes are one of the most frequent causes for trouble, so let's go over them in detail. Fig. 4-4 shows

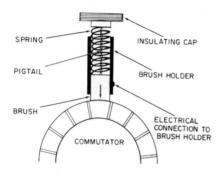

Fig. 4-4. An enlarged view of a typical brush-holder assembly.

an enlarged drawing of a typical brush and holder, and a segment of the armature. The brush is made of a carbon compound designed to make the best electrical contact with the commutator and give the least abrasive action. The brushes are mounted in a rectangular metal tube which is insulated from the motor frame, and electrical contact to the brush is made through this holder. Each brush should fit snugly in its holder, but must never bind or drag. The best check for fit is to see if it falls out of the holder when held upside down. It should "just barely" do so, yet have hardly any side play in the holder. Too much side play will allow the brush to chatter as the motor runs, creating excessive arcing and noise.

A spring holds the brush against the commutator, as shown in Fig. 4-4. Inside the spring is a stranded soft copper "pigtail" which carries the current to the brush. The pigtail should always be checked each time a brush is removed, and replaced if broken. Otherwise the spring will have to carry the current and as a result will overheat, causing it to lose its temper and tension, and the brush to bounce.

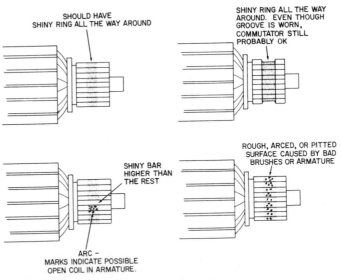

Fig. 4-5. Typical commutator conditions that result from wear and/or motor defects.

The condition of the brushes will determine the condition of the commutator, and vice versa. Both should always be examined each time an appliance is checked. Fig. 4-5 shows four typical conditions found in commutators. A normal commutator is smooth and shiny where the brushes make contact, and is always the same color all around. When the motor is running, only a very small amount of sparking should be seen underneath the ends of the brushes. Excessive sparking is always a sign of trouble—either present or coming up very soon!

Pull both brushes and check the ends; they should be very smooth. The brush should be long enough to make proper contact. The length varies, but should be about half the depth of the brush holder. Spring tension should be sufficient to hold the brush firmly but not too tightly against the commutator. Check the pigtail visually for continuity. If it is broken, the spring will show obvious signs of overheating—usually it will turn a pinkish color and lose almost all tension.

Although it's best to use exact replacement types, oversize brushes can be carefully ground down to the proper fit by rubbing back and forth across a piece of emery paper placed on a flat working surface. Frequently try the brush for fit.

Commutator Troubles

A typical commutator is shown in Fig. 4-6. The groove worn around the commutator by the brushes is all right, provided that the grooved surface is smooth all the way around. If the groove is too deep for proper contact, the commutator surface can be smoothed—but only by an expert. This is done by chucking the armature in a lathe and taking a very fine cut off the commutator surface. (Caution: This can only be done once or twice!) After the surface is smoothed, the mica spacers between the commutator bars must be filed down with the end of a fine hacksaw blade so they will be below the surface of the commutator. (Note that the mica on the commutator shown is still below the surface, despite the wear.)

Fig. 4-6. An example of a worn commutator. Although the brushes have worn a groove into the surface, the motor will probably still work properly if the rest of it is in good condition.

Fig. 4-6 also shows the slots in which the armature coils are wound. The lead wires from the coils can be seen coming out of the slots and going to the ends of the commutator segments (the light-colored area inside the ends of each bar).

Always check the ends of the commutator bars when testing an armature, especially if the motor has been overheating. If overloaded for too long, it will "throw solder," as will be apparent from close inspection. In many instances, overheating is due to a ground or short circuit inside the armature windings. Check the continuity of the windings by measuring (high range on an ohmmeter) from the commutator to the core; this circuit should be completely open. Next, use the low range of an ohmmeter to measure the continuity between each bar; the reading should be the same all around the commutator. An open circuit or a drastic change in the reading indicates a defective coil, and the armature will have to be rewound or replaced. In a few remote instances, you may spot an obviously open wire on the end of a bar and be able to resolder it successfully. Most of the time, though, any resoldering done on the commutator will throw the armature off balance and cause further trouble. So leave any such major repairs to motor specialists, or replace the armature. A new one for a small motor isn't prohibitively expensive, especially since it will save you more time and money to replace than to repair it.

Let's assume the armature is good, but there is too much sparking at the brushes while the motor is running. Obviously, new brushes and thorough cleaning of the commutator is needed. See that the new brushes fit into the holders properly, and that there is enough spring tension. Turn the motor on, and let it run for three or four minutes. Ordinarily you'll note fairly heavy sparking at the brushes during the first few moments; the reason is that most replacement brushes are square and must be "run in" on the commutator. Let the motor run until the sparking eases up a little. Stop the motor and remove the brushes—their ends should now be smooth and concave.

Use a thin strip of very fine sandpaper to smooth off the surface of the commutator. (Never use emery cloth unless you're prepared to spend some time cleaning the conductive abrasive out of the slots!) The easiest way is to wrap a piece of sandpaper around the end of a thin wooden stick; then, with the motor running, hold the sandpaper against the commutator until the surface is smooth. If you do much motor work, it'll be worth your while to buy a supply of *Sand-stick, Chalk-stick,* etc., from an electrical-supply house. This is a mild abrasive made in small sticks and looks like square chalk. It is very convenient for such work and gives a high polish to a commutator.

After cleaning the commutator, check the brushes. If properly run in, they should show contact over the entire end. Normally, you'll also note featheredging (a sharp edge on the long ends of the brush). Be sure to remove it with a piece of sandpaper before reinstalling the brushes.

BEARINGS

Bearings are another source of trouble in small motors. The great majority use a simple sleeve bearing with a tiny oil hole, mounted in a cage or rack, with a felt wick around it. Lubrication is accomplished by saturation of the felt with a light oil, which then works its way into the bearing as needed.

More trouble is caused by overoiling than by underoiling (particularly if the motor is at all accessible). However, if the motor is enclosed, such as in a mixer, it may have been used for eight or ten years without having been oiled at all! The condition of the bearings can be checked by moving the armature shaft up and down. If any play is noted, they should be replaced. Worn bearings allow the armature to bounce from side to side as it rotates, which may cause sparking, rapid brush wear, and noise.

Quite a few smaller motors have a bearing consisting simply of a brass ball with a hole in it, as shown in Fig. 4-7. Steel spring clips hold the bearing in the end-bell of the motor so it is free to move around. This allows it to be self-aligning and prevents the small

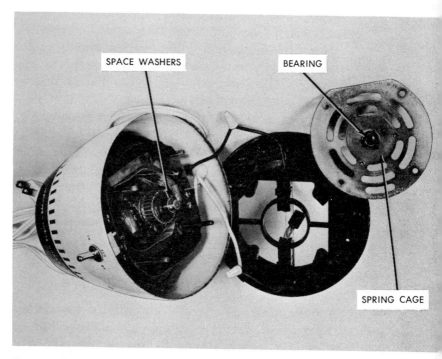

Fig. 4-7. The "captive-ball" type of bearing used on numerous small electric motors. The spring "cage" holds the ball tightly, but allows it to run at any angle necessary so that the bearing lines up correctly with the shaft. Be sure to replace all spacer washers on the motor shaft, to prevent excessive end-play.

armature from binding. These bearings also are provided with an oil wick for lubrication. To align a bearing of this type properly after a motor has been torn down and reassembled, tighten the bolts (but not too firmly) holding the motor together. Turn the armature shaft by hand until it spins almost freely. Tap the motor frame smartly on one side and the other, using a small hammer or the handle of a heavy screwdriver, until the brass ball aligns itself with the shaft and allows the armature to turn freely. Then tighten the bolts firmly and the job is done.

Incidentally, the armature in all small motors should turn freely. To check, remove the brushes and spin the armature by snapping it with your finger and thumb. It should spin for quite a while before stopping. If it is dragging, find out why (dry bearings, rough shaft, etc.) and remedy it. In some rare instances the shafts may have been scored due to lack of lubrication, corrosion, etc., inside the bearings. The only cure is to replace the armature; otherwise, the scored shaft will only ruin the new bearings you'll have to put in. Because of the small clearances, you won't have enough room to turn down the shaft and install an undersize bearing (a worthwhile procedure on a larger, more expensive motor).

CLEANING A MOTOR

A lot of motors will have several years' accumulation of flour, dust, lint, batter—you name it and you'll probably find it! If heavy enough, this encrustation may have worked its way between the armature and frame and be dragging on the motor. To remedy, disassemble the motor and clean out only the most essential places, such as the clearance between armature and frame, the bearings and brushes, and ventilation openings. It isn't usually wise to clean the whole motor; and be very careful, especially if you have to scrape dirt from around the motor windings. Use wooden or plastic tools, and never use water or any form of cleaning fluid. Either can damage the insulation or wash away any remaining lubrication in the bearings. Its best just to scrape away as much foreign matter as you can and let the rest go.

A soft brush and a couple of old toothbrushes are a great help. The end of the toothbrush handle can be carved into a paddle or point to aid in prying dirt from cracks and close places. If dirty or corroded, the shafts and bearings can be washed with a solvent—*after* the motor has been disassembled. Wipe dry and relubricate the bearings before reassembling.

CONTROLLABLE-SPEED MOTORS

Quite a few appliances, such as mixers and fans, require variable-speed motors. Some of the older fans

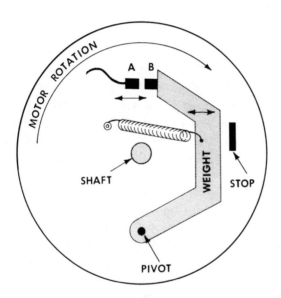

Fig. 4-8. The centrifugal speed-control mechanism used on some electric motors.

used a tapped inductor or resistor to cut down the voltage to the motor and thereby' control the speed. Today's lower-priced or simpler appliances often use this tap principle. Some of the light hand mixers have only three speeds, for example. But for maximum use-

107

fulness, the control should provide a smooth and continuous change in speed.

The centrifugal speed regulator fulfills this demand; it functions both as a manual speed control, and also as an automatic regulator to maintain a constant motor speed under varying loads in the following manner: Attached to the end of the armature is an insulated plate and an off-center pivoted arm. As the plate rotates, centrifugal force throws it away from the axis (Fig. 4-8). It is pulled back by a spring, and a stop limits its travel away from the axis.

On one end of this arm is a contact (B), and another contact (A) is fixed to a stationary plate. These contacts are usually connected in the field circuit of the motor and coupled through a pair of slip rings on the underside of the plate. Contact A is adjustable with respect to the resting position of contact B. B's position is determined by the setting of the speed-control knob. The operating current for the motor is applied through these two contacts, so that by breaking them, the speed-control knob also serves as an on-off switch.

The action of this control is as follows: When the motor starts, centrifugal force throws the arm away from the axis, breaking the contact. When the motor slows down to the desired speed, the spring pulls the arm back again, making contact and re-energizing the motor. The armature builds up speed, throwing the arm away, opening the contacts, and slowing down the motor. This action is repeated as long as power is applied to the motor. Obviously, the closer the two contacts are set (by the manual speed control), the shorter the break-and-make time of the contacts and therefore the faster the motor will run. If the control knob is turned to full speed, the contacts remain closed and the motor develops maximum speed. So, it is proper to say that the speed of the motor depends

CAPACITOR

SPEED CONTROL SHAFT

Fig. 4-9. End view of a controlled-speed motor, showing the controlling mechanism.

on the length of time the contacts remain closed during one revolution.

This may sound like the motor operates in "jerks," with power being applied and cut off so suddenly. Actually it doesn't, because of the speed at which this action takes place. At high speeds the contacts may open and close several times during one revolution, resulting in a smooth motor speed.

In practically all controls of this type, a capacitor is connected across the contacts to reduce sparking. Fig. 4-9 shows a typical motor using such a control, with the capacitor plainly visible. These are specially-made paper capacitors with small button contacts on each end that fit into brackets on the controller.

The shaft at the top of Fig. 4-9 is the speed control; the knob is fastened to it by means of a screw. As the shaft is turned it changes the distance between the contacts. Incidentally, if this motor looks a little dirty in the photograph, the reason is that it had just come in for servicing and this is how most motors look when first opened!

SAFETY PRECAUTIONS

One item that must always be checked *very* carefully before you consider an appliance fully repaired is accidental grounding of the windings to the motor or ap-

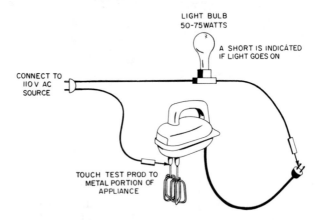

Fig. 4-10. One method of checking for a short between the motor or appliance frame and the AC line.

pliance frame. Such an oversight could cause a serious or even fatal shock, because most appliances are used on or near sinks, within easy reach of well-grounded waterpipes. A small tester can be assembled from a 50-

watt lamp, a socket, and a pair of wires with test prods, as shown in Fig. 4-10. Connect one prod to the line cord and the other to the frame of the appliance. The light will go on if there is a ground (short) between the AC line and the frame of the motor or appliance.

CHAPTER 5

APLIANCE SERVICING AS A BUSINESS

If you plan to make a profitable business out of appliance servicing, you would be wise to invest in two things—the tools of the trade, and a stock of most-needed replacement parts. The first part of this final chapter discusses various applications for specific types of tools, and the last part tells you something about where and how to obtain replacement parts.

TIME-SAVING TOOLS

In the appliance servicing business, time is money; thus the faster a job is completed, the more profitable it will be. By taking advantage of the many time-saving hand tools available, you'll be away ahead of the game. Fig. 5-1 shows just a few such tools.

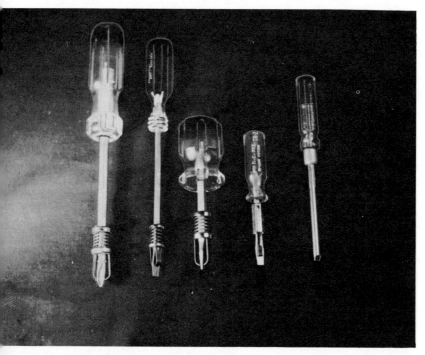

Fig. 5-1. Some screw-holding screwdrivers. At the extreme left is the outside-clip type for Phillips screws. The inside grip, at the extreme right, being no bigger than the screw, will fit into tight places which are often too snug for the outside-clip type.

Screw-holding screwdrivers are great time savers in appliance work, especially where there are many tight places in which screws must be started. There are two basic types, the outside clip and the inside grip—and each has its own particular application. For Phillips screws, the outside-clip type, seen at the left in Fig. 5-1, is almost essential.

Shown at the right is the inside-grip holder, which is made in several sizes to fit the slots of standard screw heads. The end of the blade is split, and as the handle is pushed down, the central portion of the blade turns, wedging the split ends of the blade against the sides

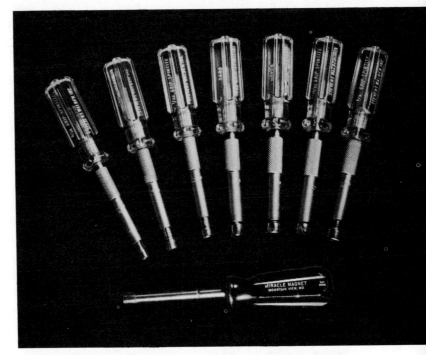

Fig. 5-2. A group of nut holders. The sliding collar holds the bolt or nut in place until inserted. The smaller wrench at the bottom of the picture has a small permanent magnet inside the socket, and the plastic shaft is spring-loaded so the bolts can be pushed out of the socket.

of the slot. The major advantage of this type of driver is that it is no bigger than the screw; if the screw can go into the available space, so can the holder. On the other hand, the outside-clip type is sometimes too big to fit into a narrow space.

Fig. 5-2 shows another handy group of tools, called nut holders. They are exactly like standard hex-nut drivers, except the socket is split lengthwise and is slightly larger than the size marked. It is slipped over the hex-head bolt or nut, and a sliding collar wedges the two halves together, gripping the nut or bolt very tightly. One distinct advantage of the nut holder is its strength. Because of its heavily-constructed collar and socket, it will tighten nuts and bolts almost as snugly as a standard socket wrench.

The smaller wrench in Fig. 5-2 has a tiny permanent magnet inside the socket. A spring-loaded plastic shaft extending through the handle is used to push small nuts out of the wrench after removal, or to hold short bolts far enough down in it for them to start. Its only disadvantage is its inability to hold nonmagnetic nuts or bolts, such as the small brass nuts used on some appliances.

Small open-end and box-end wrenches are often useful in appliance work, especially where there isn't enough clearance above the nut to allow use of a nut driver. These wrenches can be purchased separately or in sets at auto-supply stores—just ask for ignition wrenches. Buy the type with broached sockets, rather than the stamped-out types which don't last as long.

You'll probably find use for several small punches and chisels, also available at auto-supply stores in a large assortment of shapes and sizes. It's best to wait until you've done a few jobs before buying any tools, and as you need, say, a certain size of punch or chisel, then buy one. In only a short while you'll have just what you need for most jobs.

You probably won't need a full set of taps and dies, since most appliances use only a few popular sizes such as 8/32 or 10/32. The increasing use of the self-tapping or "sheet-metal" screw has eliminated much of the tedious tapping and threading formerly required.

A small tapered hand reamer, from 1/8 to 1/2 or 5/8 inch in size, can be very useful. It is available from mail-order and plumbing-supply houses, and comes in two types—one for use in a hand brace like carpenters use, and the other with a T-shaped handle for hand use.

Power Tools

Power tools such as a drill press or lathe are seldom essential, although there are a few occasions when they come in handy. However, a 1/4-inch electric drill with its various attachments can be used for a multitude of appliance repair jobs. A complete set of high-grade twist drills is almost a necessity. However, drilling holes isn't all a drill can do; clamped in a vise, it can be used to turn an arbor that will hold a small grinding wheel, a cloth wheel for polishing, or a wire wheel (a wire brush, sometimes called a scratch wheel) for cleaning and buffing. For such jobs, this handy tool can save many hours of tedious hand work. Some manufacturers

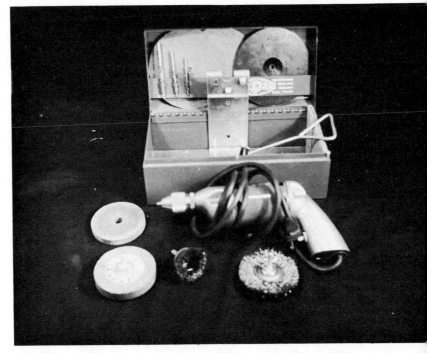

Fig. 5-3. A typical 1/4-inch drill set with attachments for buffing, sanding, and sawing as well as drilling.

have kits like the one in Fig. 5-3, which includes the drill motor with a standard chuck, plus attachments for buffing, sanding, and even sawing.

A most useful addition to your tool chest is a hand grinder, which generally includes an assortment of tiny grinding wheels, burrs much like those used by dentists, etc. This is a very handy tool for working in tight places—for example, for grinding off the ends of rivets in places where the larger drill does not reach. The small burrs will do a good job of cleaning small metal parts, grinding off nicks, straightening edges, and the like. They can also be used to ream out a hole when it is too small for the bolt.

Sanding discs, grinding wheels, burrs, and even drill bits can be purchased at auto-supply and similar stores. In fact, your dentist may be glad to give you some discarded burrs and bits, which are too dull for his work but can still be highly useful to you.

A small- to medium-sized vise is a very handy item, especially one with a rotating base. This allows you to turn the job to the most convenient angle as you work. Some sort of anvil is also useful. A piece of old iron fastened securely to the bench makes a good one. Or a piece of heavy angle iron 1½ to 2 feet long, turned over the edge of the bench and fastened down with bolts or screws, will serve as a handy anvil and also as a backing for punching rivets or similar jobs.

By drilling different-sized holes in the iron, you can use it and a punch to remove rivets. Set the rivet in the hole closest in size to that of the rivet head. Then use a pin punch with a flat end exactly the size of the rivet shank to drive the rivet through the metal. Never use a center or pointed punch; it will expand the shank of the rivet and thus enlarge the hole in the sheet metal. This makes it necessary to replace the old rivet with a larger one, which can be very unsightly.

When replacing rivets, use only a flat-headed punch or a smooth-faced hammer. To peen the end of a rivet properly, use a series of light taps rather than a few heavy swats, for a much better looking and more durable job. Use the same method when you must resort to a flat-end punch to reach a rivet—light taps until the rivet shank is peened over and held securely.

Chemical Aids

Various chemical products will be very useful for cleaning contacts, cementing parts, insulating wiring, etc. Be careful, though, not to use acetates and acrylates —which are flammable—around very hot parts of an appliance.

Penetrating oils and rust solvents are specially useful in most appliances, since one of your worst headaches is rusted or corroded nuts and bolts that won't come out. Chemical rust solvents are a great help because most nuts and bolts are so small and are made from such comparatively delicate materials (cast aluminum housings, sheet-metal parts, etc.) that you can't use force to loosen them, for fear of damaging the appliance.

When you run into a balky nut or bolt, apply the chemical solvent (sold under such trade names as *Rust-Off, Liquid Wrench, or Nut-Buster,* etc.) and let it stand overnight. The next day, the rusty nut or bolt will be much more likely to come loose.

When Chemicals Won't Work

A few special tricks will be helpful when a chemical solvent won't loosen the nut or bolt. Then mechanical methods can be tried, but you'll have to be very careful. If the screw has a standard slot, be sure the screwdriver is sharpened to the correct shape, and that it fits the slot. For best results, the screwdriver must be ground as shown in Fig. 5-4A. If the angle is too short (Fig.

119

5-4B), or if ground too sharp (Fig. 5-4C), the blade will ride up out of the slot and round off the edges, making it almost impossible to remove the screw. If someone else has already rounded off the screw, throw it away. Never re-use a badly damaged screw or bolt; you're just piling up trouble for the next guy—who just might be you!

*(A) The correct way—a long, gentle angle;
an exactly square tip; and sharp edges.*

*(B) The tip is too blunt—it will "ride up"
out of the slot and ruin the screw.*

*(C) Fine for chisels, but not for screwdrivers!
It, too, will jump out of the slot and mutilate the screw head.*

Fig. 5-4. How, and how not, to grind the tip of a screwdriver.

Damaged screw slots can sometimes be sharpened enough for the screw to be removed. A set of pattern files is very helpful, or use the sanding disc on a hand grinder. If the screw head is inaccessible with the file or hand grinder, grind a screwdriver to the exact size, place it in the slot, and tap it with a hammer. This will sometimes reshape the slot enough to allow removal of the screw.

When its head is broken completely off, or when it's so badly damaged that normal removal is impossible, the screw or bolt must be drilled out. A screw extractor

—a specially-shaped device with a left-handed thread—
is useful here. A hole is drilled through the top of the
screw or bolt, and the extractor is screwed into it. As
the extractor is turned, its left-handed thread forces it
down into the hole, so that the bolt can be turned with
it and thus be extracted.

If an extractor is not available, or if space prevents
its use, select a bit slightly smaller in diameter than
the bolt shank. Carefully center-punch the end of the
broken bolt and drill straight down into the shank.
Correctly done, this will cut out all of the jammed bolt
except part of its threads; yet the threads in the hole
will be almost undamaged, if you're careful. The hole
can be rethreaded if damaged by the bit. When a nut
and bolt are used and the hole is not threaded, the head
of the bolt can be chiseled or ground off and the shank
driven through the hole with a flat-ended punch.

PARTS PROCUREMENT

One of the biggest problems in appliance servicing
is procurement of replacement parts. Unlike many other
devices—such as radio and TV sets—most appliance replacement parts will fit only a few makes, and sometimes only one. However, the situation is not completely
impossible.

In most large cities there are several appliance parts
supply houses within easy reach. Often, in medium-
sized cities, major manufacturers or independent suppliers have set up branch offices where you can buy
locally. In small towns, however, because no local
source of supply is usually available, you will probably
have to depend on mail-order service. Few locations
are more than 100 miles from an appliance parts distributor; in fact, there is usually a choice of four or five
within this range.

So the problem boils down to one of availability and transportation. Because of road and rail schedules, quite often the city nearest you geographically is the farthest away in terms of time required for deliveries. But let's talk about procurement of parts, and come back to delivery in a minute. In general, there are two sources for obtaining parts: first, the state distributor for the maker of the appliance in question. He is usually located in the state's largest city, but may have branch offices in other cities if demand warrants it. Your second source is the independent appliance parts wholesaler, who handles parts for all major appliances. His offices will also be located in the largest or most centrally located city in the state.

Usually, the independent wholesaler is a much faster and more reliable source of replacement parts than the state distributor for that brand, possibly because the excessive paper work necessary in the manufacturer's operations slows down delivery. Another problem is confusion about part numbers: manufacturers often turn down an order for a part, stating "there is no such number," even though the number is stamped right on the part. Exhaustive catalogs, issued by many appliance parts wholesalers, may help to solve this problem, since they not only list parts for all appliances, but also cross reference between models and manufacturers.

Sometimes a manufacturer will market the identical appliance under two different brand names. Moreover, even though the units are identical they may carry different part numbers. As a result, parts ordered from one are often refused with the suggestion that the order be sent to the alternate "manufacturer." To add to the confusion, the latter sometimes refers you to the one you wrote to originally!

So your first step in getting started in the appliance repair business is to contact other appliance service shops in your area and find out from whom they have the best luck in getting replacement parts. You may find that in your community the appliance distributor, not the parts wholesaler, gives better service.

If you must rely on mail delivery, you should check the train and bus schedules and the times of mail deliveries. Most important, find out when each carrier leaves the city where the parts are ordered. In an actual example, the supply city was 90 miles away and mail left there twice a day, at 4:00 A.M. and 5:00 P.M. By mail order it was possible to get parts the next day if ordered in the morning, because mail went in that direction on a noon train. For really fast delivery, a bus left the city at 12:15 P.M. and arrived at 3:00 P.M. the same day. So parts could be ordered by telephone in the morning and picked up that afternoon. It is helpful to make up a chart showing the latest possible times you could call long distance and still get a part the same day.

If a part is unobtainable from any nearby sources, you will have to order directly from the factory, and you can count on a delay of several days, or even weeks, for delivery. For emergency repairs where cost is a minor item, telephoning the factory service manager and requesting shipment by Air Express will usually get you quicker service than ordering by letter. Often a telegram will work. For the same rate as a day letter, night letters allow you to use more words and hence longer descriptions of the part, yet with only a few hours' lag in delivery time.

How many parts to stock is determined by your volume of appliance business and the nearness of suppliers. Of course, you should stock as many as possible, in order not to waste time running after parts—but within limits. Because of rapid obsolescence and the lack of interchangeability, you can easily accumulate a large and expensive collection of "dogs." The best way, for the first few months, is to carry only the minimum stock of parts and note which ones you use most. Then a small stock of these can be laid in. Later, as your business grows, others can be added. Of course, universal parts such as line cords, appliance plugs, and the like can be purchased immediately and in fairly large quantities, since all appliances can use them.

One method of obtaining fairly rapid delivery of parts, if you plan to engage heavily in the appliance business, is to contact as many well-known manufacturers as possible and ask for an appointment as a factory-authorized service station for their line. If you secure a go-ahead, make the rounds of all appliance dealers within your trade area and let them know you now have this authorization. Many will gladly give you all their warranty replacement work, and in this way you can build up your volume of appliance business to the point where it will be more worth your while to carry an adequate stock of replacement parts.

One last word about parts procurement: Customers are often impatient to have an appliance repaired. For some reason, they don't mind waiting a reasonable length of time, *as long as you deliver when promised!* But if they have to wait one more day, you're in deep trouble! Customers in smaller towns don't seem to be as demanding as those in larger cities; they're accustomed to waiting and as a rule are quite patient. For the "can't wait" customer who must have the job done immediately, tell him or her that you'll be very happy to oblige—but there will be a small extra charge for long-distance telephone calls, bus charges, etc. Tell him how much—he may change his mind and give you all the time you need.

GLOSSARY

A

Armature—That portion of a motor (usually the rotating member) that includes the main current-carrying winding.

Asbestos—A fibrous fireproof material used in heater cords, and in other applications where excessive heat may present a fire hazard.

Auxiliary Switch—A switch used to support another one in the performance of a desired function.

B

Bimetal Blade—A blade used primarily in thermostats. It is comprised of two dissimilar metals, one having a high expansion rate as it is heated, and the other a low expansion rate.

Brick—A molded ceramic form on which the heating element of an appliance is mounted. Sometimes the element is embedded in the brick.

Brush—A carbon or metal block that provides electrical contact with the rotating member of an electrical device (for example, a motor or generator).

Brush Chatter—A condition that exists when the commutator on a motor armature is out of round or has a rough or uneven surface, causing the brushes to bounce as the armature rotates.

Bypass Capacitor—A component used in a number of motor-operated household appliances to reduce arcing and/or to suppress noise which could interfere with radio and TV reception.

C

Cam—A rotating or sliding lever used to give complicated and precisely timed movements in a machine or engine.

Capacitor—A component comprised of two conductors separated by an insulating material known as the dielectric.

Centrifugal Speed Regulator—A device which governs the speed of a motor by utilizing the force that tends to impel an object outward from its center of rotation.

Ceramic—A nonconducting material commonly used as a mounting for heating elements, or in feedthrough insulators, etc.

Commutator—That portion of an armature comprised of copper segments against which the brushes make contact.

Conductor—A material that offers little or no opposition to the flow of electric current.

Contacts—Two circular pieces of hardened steel mounted on supporting conductors, used to provide intermittent connection between circuits, or between different parts of the same circuit.

Continuity—The property of having a continuous DC electrical path.

Current Drain—The amount of current drawn from a source.

E

Eccentric Cam—A cam having unequal radii. (See *Cam*.)

Electromagnetic Field—A combination of electric and magnetic fields produced by the flow of electric current through a wire or coil.

Electromechanical Device—A device that is both mechanical and electrical, such as an automatic toaster.

F

Feedthrough Insulator—A tubular insulator (usually made of ceramic) inserted into a hole through which a conductor must pass. It is used to keep the conductor from shorting against the sides of the hole.

Field Coil—The coils that produce the magnetic field in a motor.

G

Grommet—An insulating washer, usually made of rubber or plastic, inserted into a metal hole to prevent a wire or cable from scraping against the sides of the hole.

Ground—The neutral, or low, side of a power line or an appliance. In the latter, the frame is considered ground.

Growler—An electromagnetic device used for locating defective coils in an armature. It derives its name from the growling noise produced as the armature is rotated within its jaws.

H

Heater Cord—A heavy-duty two-conductor cord designed primarily for home appliances requiring large amounts of power, such as irons, "hot plates," etc.

Heating Element—A low-resistance wire which becomes very hot as a result of its opposition to current flowing through it.

High-Resistance Connection—A connection that offers a large opposition to the flow of electric current. This can be caused by a connection being loose, corroded, rusted, etc.

Housing—A protective device which surrounds the working components of a motor, appliance, etc.

I

Ignition Wrenches—Small open or box-end wrenches used primarily for working on ignition systems, radios, etc.

Insulation—A nonconducting material used to prevent a current from taking undesired paths as it flows through a conductor.

Interlock Plug—A plug that automatically becomes disconnected from the circuit when disassembly of a device is begun.

K

Kilowatt—1000 watts.

L

Laminated—Being made up of layers, such as the laminated core of a coil.

Line Cord—A two-conductor wire terminated with a two-prong plug, used for connecting to a wall outlet.

M

Magnetic Contacts—A set of contacts that are snapped together by magnetic attraction when a specified distance apart. They prevent arcing that would otherwise occur if the contacts were to come together slowly.

Magnetic Field—The immediate area, around a magnet or a current-carrying conductor or coil, where magnetic lines of force exist.

Mechanism—The mechanical parts, in a device, needed to perform its intended function.

Mica—A material with excellent insulating and heat-resisting properties. Mica insulating washers are often used around and under electrical terminals on household appliances.

N

Neon Lamp—A small neon-filled lamp used as an indicating device on a number of appliances. Applying a voltage of the correct value causes the gas within the lamp to glow.

O

Ohm—The unit of resistance.

Ohmmeter—An instrument used to measure resistance.

Ohm's Law Formula—The formula that expresses the relationship between voltage, current, and resistance—for example $I = E \div R$ is one.

Open—A circuit or component in which the electrical path is no longer continuous.

Oven Thermometer—A special thermometer used to check high temperatures in an oven, rotisserie, etc.

P

Pattern File—A small fine-toothed file.

Permanent Magnet—A piece of metal that retains its magnetism after the magnetizing force has been removed.

Phillips Screw—A screw with an + instead of a slot in the head.

"Pigtail"—A braided copper wire fastened to the end of a brush to provide contact between the brush and the rest of the circuit.

Power Source—The source from which a device receives its power, such as a wall outlet, battery, etc.

R

Receptacle—A socket or other outlet into which a plug can be inserted to make electrical contact.

Resistance Wire—A wire that becomes very hot due to its high opposition to the flow of electrical current. It is used principally as a heating element in household appliances.

Revolution—One complete turn around an axis.

Rivet—A soft metal pin or bolt used to unite two or more pieces of metal.

Rotary Switch—A switch having its contacts mounted in a circle.

S

Safetied Splice—A splice that has been secured with additional material to insure maximum strength and thus safety.

Screw Extractor—A device used for removing "frozen" or broken screws.

GLOSSARY

Self-tapping Screw—A tapered screw, made of hard metal, that forms its own threads as it is driven into a material.

Setscrew—A screw having a hexagonal hole through its center, in place of a head. A hexagonal L-shaped tool known as an Allen wrench is inserted in the hole to loosen or tighten the screw.

Silicone Grease—A grease with a higher-than-normal melting point.

Spit—A slender rod with prongs used for holding meat over a fire.

Splice—A joint between two conductors that has both mechanical strength as well as electrical conductivity.

Strain Relief—A device used to grip the line cord in order to keep strain off the electrical connections.

SV Cord—A cord comprised of two rubber-insulated conductors surrounded by a fiber lay and covered with a heavy rubber or plastic jacket.

Synchronous Motor—A motor that operates on the principle of magnetic repulsion and attraction. It requires no brushes or commutators.

T

Thermostat—A device that automatically regulates the temperature produced by a heating element. (Also see *Bimetal Blade*.)

Timer—A device that can be set to control a particular operation for a predetermined length of time.

U

Underwriter's Code—A set of electrical standards established by a group of fire and casualty insurance companies, and now adopted as a legal requirement by many cities.

V

Voltage Frequency—The number of cycles an AC voltage goes through during one second.

Voltmeter—A meter used to measure potential difference (voltage).

W

Watt—A unit of electrical power.

Wattmeter—A meter used to measure electrical power.

Wire Nut—A tapered plastic or ceramic nut that is screwed down onto a wire splice to hold it securely.

Worm Gear—A cylindrical gear with grooves similar to the threads on a bolt.

Z

Zip Cord—A stranded two-conductor wire covered with rubber or plastic and having a groove down the center to permit easy separation of the conductors.